THE HISTORY OF FORT ST. JOSEPH

The History of FORT ST. JOSEPH

John Abbott
Graeme S. Mount
Michael J. Mulloy

THE DUNDURN GROUP
TORONTO · OXFORD

Copyeditor: Barry Jowett
Design: Jennifer Scott
Maps by Daryl White, except where noted
Printer: Friesens Corporation

Canadian Cataloguing in Publication Data

Abbott, John Roblin, 1936- .
The history of Fort St. Joseph

Includes bibliographical references and index.
ISBN 1-55002-337-3
1. Fort St. Joseph (Ont.) — History. 2. Fort St. Joseph National Historic Park (Ont.).
I. Mount, Graeme S. (Graeme Stewart) 1939- . II. Mulloy, Michael J. (Michael John) 1916- .
III. Title

FC3064.F677M68 2000   971.3'132   C00-930058-9   F1059.F677A22 2000

1   2   3   4   5   04   03   02   01   00

Canada

THE CANADA COUNCIL | LE CONSEIL DES ARTS
FOR THE ARTS | DU CANADA
SINCE 1957 | DEPUIS 1957

We acknowledge the support of the **Canada Council for the Arts**, the **Ontario Arts Council**, and the **Book Publishing Industry Development Program (BPIDP)** for our publishing activities.

Dundurn Press
8 Market Street
Suite 200
Toronto, Ontario, Canada
M5E 1M6

Dundurn Press
73 Lime Walk
Headington, Oxford,
England
OX3 7AD

Dundurn Press
2250 Military Road
Tonawanda, New York,
U.S.A. 14150

THE HISTORY OF FORT ST. JOSEPH

Contents

Acknowledgements

Many people contributed to publication of this book. Frances Robb, Line Madore, and Barry Guzzo of Parks Canada at Fort St. Joseph and Dennis Carter-Edwards and Carol Phillips of Parks Canada's Ontario headquarters at Cornwall provided personal expertise, the resources of their libraries, and documentary evidence. Algoma University College and Laurentian University provided moral support, secretarial assistance, and money, particularly through the INORD programme (Institute of Northern Ontario Research and Development) at Laurentian University and CNODS (Centre for Northern Ontario Development Studies) at Algoma. Jane Pitblado at the INORD office was particularly helpful, and the secretarial work of Rose-May Démoré was, as always, indispensable. The Province of Ontario's Summer Experience Programme also provided funding, for which we are grateful. The Sault Ste. Marie Public Library willingly provided access to the extensive Glyn Smith Collection in its custody. Students Andre Laferriere, Jennifer Foreman, and Daryl White accompanied us in our travels to libraries and forts, searched for information and photocopied extensively, and observed what we might have missed. The first two of those students also provided preliminary drafts of three chapters, while the third drew maps. Algoma's Professor Bill Newbigging examined and made invaluable suggestions upon the prehistoric section, and the people at Dundurn Press committed themselves to and worked upon this book. The local media publicized our work, and in response to media coverage, Mike Spears from Dearborn, Michigan, provided documentation of which we had been unaware.

Our wives — Ruth Abbott, Joan Mount, Marjory Mulloy — accepted our frequent absences from home and our commitment to this manuscript when we were at home. To all of the above we express our appreciation. Nevertheless, any mistakes are the responsibility of the authors.

John Abbott
Graeme S. Mount
Michael J. Mulloy

Introduction

There is no shortage of good writing about the War of 1812, as a glimpse at the bibliography at the end of this book will make clear. The gap is a book about Fort St. Joseph itself: its origins, its moment of fame, its resurrection from oblivion.

Few residents of Sudbury, the nearest city east of Fort St. Joseph, have heard of the place. Indeed, it would appear that few who live outside the District of Algoma know about it. At the time of writing, there are only two signs — one for eastbound travellers, one for westbound travellers — on the Trans-Canada Highway (Highway 17) to alert motorists to the existence of a historic site maintained by Parks Canada on St. Joseph Island. There is only one such sign for eastbound travellers. Most casual observers of the War of 1812 are aware that British military victories on Mackinac Island in 1812 and 1814 assured British control of the Upper Great Lakes, and Pierre Berton's *The Invasion of Canada*[1] describes the fort and the people who lived there in 1812.

Unfortunately, although quite understandably, Berton is almost unique. Most writers about the war have noted the victory at Mackinac, and then focused on the Niagara Peninsula, where considerably more fighting took place. The fact that most writers have lived in Southern Ontario, close to the Niagara Peninsula but a day's drive from St. Joseph Island, may also have contributed to this reality.

Those who prepared this book are residents of Sudbury and Sault Ste. Marie, who feel that the story of Fort St. Joseph deserves more attention than it has received. Residents of northeastern Ontario as well as tourists to the area should know that a British military outpost once flourished in their neighbourhood. They should be aware of its achievements and its demise. They should know that in the twentieth century, public-spirited lobbyists from the District of Algoma persuaded the appropriate authorities to excavate what remained of the buildings and to create a historic park with something of interest for the entire family. History buffs can stand amid the ruins and imagine a pocket of European culture located hundreds of kilometres from the base at Lachine on Montreal Island. They can reconstruct (figuratively) the fur trade, in which both First Nations peoples and Europeans participated. They can appreciate the accomplishments of those who set forth across Lake Huron in 1812 to capture Fort Mackinac, and they can understand the frustration of the American arsonists who torched Fort St. Joseph in 1814. The museum operated by Parks Canada helps place the site into context, as do films shown at the theatre. Children can run and play amid the ruins, and even the family dog can enjoy a walk. Swimming facilities, picnic sites, campgrounds, and a bird sanctuary are within walking distance, and on certain August evenings, Fort St. Joseph offers ghost walks. Residents of the District of Algoma dress in period costume, traverse the ruins, and re-enact scenes of almost two hundred years ago.

A conviction that tourists are interested in more than campgrounds and casinos prompted the preparation of this book. Surely some residents of northeastern Ontario would spend part of their vacation in the area, especially during the warmest weeks of summer, if they knew they could visit its historic sites — especially a site as beautiful as Fort St. Joseph. Surely some of the millions of tourists travelling through the District of Algoma on the Trans-Canada Highway would spend more time in the area if they were aware of the availability of a historic site of this nature.

There is not a mountain of information in these pages that is not accessible elsewhere. What this book does is collate the information into one handy volume for the tourist or amateur historian with limited time. Hopefully the book can attract tourists to Fort St. Joseph and serve as a souvenir for those who have visited it.

John Abbott, Algoma University College, Sault Ste. Marie
Jennifer Foreman, Algoma University College, Sault Ste. Marie
Andre Laferriere, Laurentian University, Sudbury
Graeme S. Mount, Laurentian University, Sudbury
Michael J. Mulloy, Sudbury
Daryl White, Laurentian University, Sudbury
December 1999

Prologue

The Upper Great Lakes Context —
St. Joseph Island Before Construction of the Fort

St. Joseph Island is but a blip on the moving screen of geological history. Even on the scale of the geologists' professional interest it had scarcely registered, for the first serious study of the island's glacial shorelines was initiated only in 1980. The mapping of its sand and gravel deposits followed in 1981 and 1982. For historians and others who wish to understand the relationships between the land and its human occupants, these recent studies are helpful. They explain why what developed consisted largely of glaciers that deposited their contents, and a succession of glacial lakes that sorted and shaped those deposits into the features that characterize the island today.

The last ice lobe to claim the territory extended as far south as a line cutting lower northern Michigan and the adjacent basin of what is now Lake Huron. As it began its retreat some 11,000 years ago, the vast volume of melt-water that streamed from its margins sustained Lake Algonquin, a

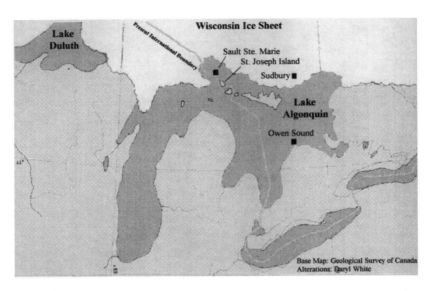

As the glaciers began to recede during the last ice age, the present-day location of Sault Ste. Marie was beneath the giant Lake Algonquin, while St. Joseph Island, formed by glacial debris, emerged.

body of water so deep at its greatest extent that only the very top of "The Mountain" — now some 13 kilometres north and 160 metres above the level of Fort St. Joseph — stood above the icy inland sea. This vast and very deep accumulation of glacial debris was deposited between some 30,000 and 11,000 years ago, rendering St. Joseph Island a newly minted arrival on the glacial scene.[1] Between 5,000 and 11,000 years ago as ice dams melted and the land, relieved of the great weight of the ice, rebounded, new outlets for the impoundments were created and new lake levels were established. At one very low-water point in the process (the Lake Stanley stage of development), the island was considerably larger than at present, and a far more turbulent St. Mary's River extended well into territory now covered by Lake Huron.[2] Meanwhile, as the island emerged from its glacial womb, the waters retreated and advanced, shaping and abandoning shore lines, cutting water courses, and depositing soils of many kinds into deep and shallow waters. Finally, between 5,000 and 3,000 years ago, St. Joseph Island assumed a form similar to its present configuration, its resources available for exploitation as human requirements dictated and technology permitted.[3]

Intriguing as it may be to contemplate, any understanding of Aboriginal occupation and use of the island's resources over the last several millennia rests more upon speculation than knowledge. In contrast to the islands in and land bordering the Strait of Mackinac, St. Joseph Island and its environs were lightly used and occupied only seasonally. Thin, rather acidic soils, frost, flood, and an ever-active forest environment combined to destroy animal and vegetable evidence of human habitation. Archaeological remains are accordingly scanty, scattered, and unattractive to professionals seeking evidence of depth and long-term occupation. Knowledge of the island's human activity before the seventeenth century is therefore a product of oral transmission, the extrapolation of knowledge derived from archaeological and anthropological investigations in comparable environments elsewhere, careful interpretation of information derived from early European sources such as *Jesuit Relations*, and incidental discoveries of Aboriginal artifacts on St. Joseph Island itself.

That said, it is possible to make educated guesses about the general nature of the local environment some 11,000 years ago. The glacial lobe of what proved to be the last in a long series of glacial advances was releasing its grip on that massive load of till which is the island's legacy from the Ice Age, surrendering this vast pile of gravel to the erosive elements above and the waters of glacial Lake Algonquin below. Gradually, as ice and water receded, successions of plants found friendly environments. These, in turn, attracted grazers large and small as well as the predators that accompanied, killed, and consumed them. Among the most efficient predators were human beings, known to archaeologists and anthropologists largely through the durable part of their weapons and the tools used to fashion them.

The first human predators to traverse the ridges of St. Joseph Island may have been members of the group that anthropologists label the Plano People. Some 10,500 to 8,000 years ago, these hunters — who had probably migrated from the interior plains of North America — migrated north into that vast region between Hudson Bay and the Rocky Mountains, to the northeast into the peninsula dividing lakes Michigan and Superior, through Michigan into Ontario as far as Georgian Bay and the Severn-Trent drainage system, and ultimately northeasterly to the southern rim of the Gulf of St. Lawrence and the Atlantic coastal plain to the south of Cape Breton Island. The northeasterly limits of Plano colonization in the Upper Great Lakes region were defined by a narrow fringe bordering Lake Superior, the St. Mary's River, and the territory that now defines the North Channel of Lake Huron, including Manitoulin and St. Joseph islands. Samples of the carefully chipped, exquisitely tapered, and beautifully rippled (fluted) project points they manufactured marked their passage. Plano sites have also been discovered along the north shore of Lake Superior and on both sides of the North Channel.[4]

Like their predecessors, the original fluted-point people (11,500 to 10,200 years ago), the Plano People were meticulous in their choice of stone, searching out the best sources to quarry, selecting it for aesthetic as well as utilitarian qualities, travelling several hundred kilometres each year in their search for food. They exchanged their wares — especially their stone tools — with other small groups of hunters. Originally the Plano people had moved with and preyed upon the great herds of bison, the predominant grazer on the interior grasslands from whence people had come. As groups of these large animal hunters moved east and north in the track of the receding glacier, however, they entered forested environments more supportive of caribou and the creatures which preyed on them. Some 11,000 to 9,000 years ago, plants typical of tundra, lichen (open) woodland, and boreal forest colonized

St. Joseph Island and its environs. The caribou's seasonal round included shelter in the boreal forest during the winter and northward migration into the more lush, open lichen woodland for the summer. One would expect that the first hunters on the island were specialists in the stalking, reduction, and utilization of caribou and other large animals.[5]

While these ancient people (known collectively to archaeologists as Palaeo-Indians) were primarily hunters of large animals, their successors, the Archaic Indians — through some combination of opportunity, necessity, and preference — drew upon a much greater range of food sources, maritime as well as terrestrial. In turn, this diversification generated technological innovation and cultural pluralism. The Archaic peoples were predecessors of those people who lived in the Upper Great Lakes region when Samuel de Champlain sent Etienne Brûlé on his missions there after 1610. Yet, in many respects, scholars know less about them than about the Plano People.[6]

Demographically as well as geologically, St. Joseph Island was a borderland. The Manitoulin archipelago forms a boundary between territories occupied by the Laurentian Archaic and Shield Archaic peoples. The former, who arrived from the southeast, took possession of the lower St. Lawrence and the eastern Great Lakes basin some 8,000 to 7,000 years ago. They ranged north to a line very close to that defined by the French River-Lake Nipissing-Mattawa River axis, sustaining themselves through fishing and big-game hunting. By contrast, the Shield Archaic peoples — probably an offshoot of the Plano culture — probably migrated southeastward from regions west of the Tyrrell Sea (a larger Hudson Bay) some 7,500 years ago. They moved along the northern shores of post-glacial impoundments whose successors have become lakes Superior and Huron, no doubt adapting their fishing techniques to take advantage of the greater variety of fish sustained by the warming waters, and hunting the caribou. The Manitoulin archipelago's transitional character is evident from archaeological evidence indicating that both Late Palaeo-Indian and Early Archaic occupants (9,000 to 8,000 years ago) shared the same space.[7]

Archaeologists emphasize the diffusion of pottery and even characterize the culture of the people who inhabited a large crescent of territory between the upper Great Lakes and Hudson Bay as Laurel, in response to the northward diffusion of the potter's art some 2,500 to 1,500 years ago. However, it seems probable that the closely related cultures that ultimately characterized the lives of the Algonquian peoples who — when Europeans arrived lived on the Canadian Shield and the Hudson Bay lowlands — were basically the product of deep Archaic roots and the Canadian Shield's resource base. Their cultures rested upon different combinations of hunting, fishing, and gathering. About 1,500 years ago, agriculture began to shape the Iroquoian culture to the south. Once again, it was along the line of the Manitoulin archipelago that the two cultures met, exchanging goods, ideas, and blows.[8]

The environment of St. Joseph Island is transitional in terms of its bedrock, the glacial drift that constitutes its soil and determines its biotic complement, and the forest, whose abundant groves of deciduous trees prompted pre-European inhabitants known as the Anishinaabe people to identify it as "niibiish" or leaf(y).[9] In general, St. Joseph Island sits on the ragged outer edge of the climatic zone where corn may be cultivated with hope of a regular harvest, and beyond the safe limit for winter squash and beans — the famous "three sisters" whose presence helped differentiate Iroquoian from Algonquian cultures. There were periods in the past when the climate was either warmer or colder than at present. Immediately before and after the arrival of Europeans (roughly 1300 to 1750), the region experienced a "little ice age," when none of the three sisters could have grown on the island. (Nowadays corn from St. Joseph Island is the product of sophisticated breeding designed to shorten the period from planting to harvest, but knowledge of such rapid production is fairly recent.)

Furthermore, St. Joseph's glacial soils, derived in large measure from the rocks of the Canadian Shield to the north, tended to be somewhat more acidic and less hospitable to crops such as corn than were the sweeter, more calcareous soils farther south. When they appeared in the local diet, elements of the three sisters were incidental, often the products of trade, not the result of indigenous cultivation. Those who inhabited the island were hunters, fishers, and gatherers, not farmers. Archaeological evidence indicates that the site of Fort St. Joseph supported human activities as many as 5,000 years ago.[10] Resources available on the island and from surrounding waters may have invited periodic exploitation by small groups of Palaeo and Archaic Indians before that, but any evidence has perished or exists underwater or remains to be found.

Any examination of an island's past must include the use made of its surrounding waters. The Upper Great Lakes and their post-glacial predecessors challenged human ingenuity. Water is as much a part of an island's environment as land, sustaining food stocks, defining travel routes, and determining modes of transportation. What people make of their opportunities is determined by a mysterious mixture of human needs and wants, facility, and ingenuity, along with past practice. Reflection on any relationship between environmental challenge and human response may reveal, however imperfectly, some aspects of Anishnabeg life before the arrival of Europeans.

Logic suggests that even Palaeolithic people living in an environment where large rivers and lakes were both an impediment and an opportunity would have travelled by water. While it is impossible to determine when an innovation such as the canoe came into existence, the existence of Palaeolithic sites on lakes and rivers indicates an inclination to harvest their resources. When associated with the capacity to create and use tools, the inventive curiosity of human beings surely suggests the existence of wooden conveyances, even dugouts under appropriate circumstances. Evidence of an increasingly sophisticated wood-working tool kit indicates the possibility of bark canoes later in the Archaic period. Sophisticated fishing technologies, for which ample evidence exists in the Archaic period, also had their cruder origins in the Palaeolithic period. The learning curve was no doubt a gradual slope rather than a set of distinct steps.

The Archaic period was increasingly rich in options, possibilities that nurtured inventive genius. The bark of the birch tree was to the Algonquian peoples what buffalo hide was to the natives of the interior plains. Both materials were tough and waterproof, capable of shedding and holding water and other liquids. Both could be used for buckets, for a water- and windproof cladding on the frameworks of habitations, and for covering the ribs, stems, and gunnels of watercraft. While the semi-arid nature of the great plains did not challenge its inhabitants fully to exploit the potential of leather as a boat-building material, the opportunity to utilize the maritime resource of the Upper Great Lakes inspired the Algonquian people to combine birch-bark, cedar, and spruce in a craft remarkable for its beauty and utility.

The bark canoe probably began as a quicker, lighter version of the dugout, employing whatever bark was available and could be attached to a framework of ready-shaped, or readily shaped tree branches and withes. The bark of spruce and elm — heavy, leaky, weak, and corrugated — must for most purposes have given way to birchbark, for the birch grew great in girth and numbers in the Upper Great Lakes region. Harvesters gathered the bark itself from the living tree in the spring of the year, using the heat from a birch-bark flare to help loosen the bond between bark and wood, sharp stone tools to make the vertical and horizontal incisions, and carefully flattened and sharpened wooden paddles to separate the bark from the trunk. This they stored in rolls, white side in, until needed.

The builders first created a construction bed by clearing the litter from a flat patch of ground. Onto this bed they rolled

CANOE CONSTRUCTION

out the bark. Atop this they placed a frame, weighted with rocks and usually made of eastern white cedar. As they bent the bark upward to accommodate the curves in the hull, they drove stakes into the ground to maintain its shape. Then cedar strips were steamed and bent to form interior ribs, while thwarts and gunnels provided transverse and longitudinal stiffening to maintain the craft's efficient shape. At this point a third tree, the spruce, contributed two indispensable elements to complete the canoe's construction. Bog-grown spruce was easily pushed over, to reveal the long taproot, the source of "wattap." After boiling had softened their fibres, the roots were separated into supple withes, which the builders fed through holes in the bark and bound around all the seams in the skin and the components of the frame to create a craft storied for its durability, reparability, portability, agility, and carrying capacity. Next they waterproofed their craft by sealing the holes and seams with pitch made from boiled spruce sap. Finally, the artisans worked decorations into the canoe's flanks, and fashioned paddles from birch or cedar. Few creations better illustrate the way necessity, inspiring invention, can turn a collection of indigenous materials into an item of beauty and utility.

Water supported a fishery. From the arrival of the first people, fish must have been a staple of the local diet. Whitefish and lake trout were important, but they were deep water fish, available only during certain seasons of the year and concentrated in particular locations, such as the falls at St. Mary's and the straits at Mackinac. From the first Jesuits onward, European witnesses extolled the whitefish fishery. So vivid were descriptions of swarming schools and agile fishers that many assumed the whitefish to be ubiquitous. Nothing was further from the truth. John Askin, Indian Department Agent at Fort St. Joseph, informed his father that the run at Sault Ste. Marie would not begin until October, at which time he would negotiate with a Sault fisherman to supply him with a barrel. The following year he reported the discovery of a whitefish ground some twenty-one miles from the fort, but he observed that the fish stayed there only a short time after mid-November. An analysis of food remains at Fort St. Joseph confirms that residents ate bass and sunfish, pike and muskellunge, sturgeon, sauger, perch, suckers, and redhorses, shallow-water varieties that, taken together, constituted a reliable stock. Whitefish and cisco comprised less than 10 percent of the diet, about the same as suckers, while bass and sunfish amounted to some 26 percent.[11]

Indicative of St. Joseph Island's marginal location and environment is the reality that several of these shallow water species occupied the northern limits of their range. Longnose gar, bowfin, channel catfish, white bass, and freshwater drum are examples of warm-water fish that found aquatic conditions around the island to their liking. Others, such as the muskellunge, silver redhorse, brown bullhead, and bluegill were generally to be found no further north in Great Lakes waters. For these the extensive, relatively shallow sandy bays, moderately deep river channels, rapids, and open water found round the island offered a hospitable environment. They offered fishers a range of opportunity to harvest through the seasons, though of course they were not usually found in the seasonal concentrations that made the whitefishery at St. Mary's such an attraction.

Fishing tackle was varied and inventive. Many of the devices date to the Archaic period and were more or less concurrent with the development of the bark canoe. They included fishing nets and lines fashioned of fibrous herbaceous materials, sinkers and net weights grooved or drilled for effective fastening, as well as bone fish hooks.[12] Evidence of fishing nets appears on the surface of pottery from the early Woodland period, for pieces of netting were sometimes used to make decorative and utilitarian impressions on the surface of the pots while the clay was still malleable. Literature of the early contact period describes a variety of devices and techniques: a variety of seines (nets for catching fish) equipped with floats above and weights below, used to encompass a volume of water thought to hold fish; gill nets with mesh diameters calculated to ensnare fish of a particular size and shape; weirs or traps made of various materials, fixed in place, designed to make an entrance easy and exit difficult; spears whose length, weight, and terminal configurations varied according to the requirements of the species sought; harpoons, dip nets, even bows and arrows, as well as sticks and rocks. As a rule, nets were used for smaller fish, spears for larger ones.[13]

Food dominated the thinking of aboriginals to an extent unknown among modern people, most of whom take the food supply for granted. Opportunity did not knock every day, and they had to respond at the right moment. They familiarized themselves with the timetables of animal, bird, and fish migrations and adjusted their own travel plans accordingly. Catching and preparing fish for long-term storage required a mobilization of labour, the establishment of a fishing camp on location at the appropriate time of the year, and a focus on smoking the fillets. Any location with a reputation for producing quantities of fish over a period of years would become an habitual seasonal camp ground. The number of people the location could support depended on the concentration of the resource. Likewise, the nature of the aquatic environment determined the technology employed. Dip nets worked well when fish schooled in rapids; gill nets did not. Fishing utilized the labour of the entire family — men, women, and children. Women often caught as well as cured the fish.

The island's forest supported nut-bearing trees. Passenger pigeons returned every spring to ransack the litter of quantities of mast, acorns, and beechnuts, produced in the previous year. During the breeding season, Aboriginal gatherers made their way among the nests, collecting quantities of squab when they were at their fattest, about two weeks after emerging from the eggs. The numerous marshes round the island harboured waterfowl of many species. Their seasonal moult, which occurs in mid-to-late summer and leaves them flightless, rendered them vulnerable to herding, capture, and slaughter. The Ojibwa scooped them up in nets.

From Archaic times the sojourners in and inhabitants of this region collected a variety of plants in their seasonal quests for food. Plants and their products probably earned a more prominent place in the Aboriginal diet as the Palaeo gave way to the Archaic way of life. With the glacier's retreat, moderating climate and water temperature enhanced both the variety and concentration of land and water plants, making it worthwhile to travel to certain locations, remain to enjoy the seasonal delights, and process commodities for future use. Plants not only added vitamins to the diet; when combined with storage technology, they enhanced winter diets.

The sap run of early spring attracted campers to groves of sugar maple, box elder, and silver birch. Then as now the syrup and sugar functioned as flavouring agents, making food more palatable after winter's privations. Trees were tapped on the south side, the nectar directed by ash spigots into birch-bark buckets sewn up with withes of spruce roots and waterproofed with spruce pitch. A little later wild leeks, a treat to delight the most jaded pallet, could be collected along with the tender, newly emergent shoots of ferns. The latter, now known as fiddleheads (a fresh green), are available today only in specialty markets at a premium price. The bracken fern provided soup and medicine. Jack-in-the-pulpit tubers were both food and medicine, as were marigold and milkweed. Buds and flowers of many plants, dried and stored for winter, provided both medicine and fibre. Bullrush stems when woven became mats and baskets.

Summer and fall provided harvests of currants, raspberries, blueberries, and Canada plums. The cranberry bogs on St. Joseph Island offered an abundant and important source of food and flavouring. While soft fruits such as strawberries were best eaten out-of-hand, others could be dried and stored for winter. In fall, acorns and beechnuts were an important source of starch. However, they also

Chippewa Indian women making maple syrup near Sault Ste. Marie, 1762.
Courtesy of the Museum, Sault Ste. Marie, Ontario

served as medicine and a source of dye. Medicine was anything thought capable of altering a condition. It might be burned as incense and taken to provoke ceremonial dreams. Dye was available from husks by boiling, a process that also leached the tannin from acorns. The leaves of some plants, the bearberry for one, could be dried and smoked. One of the most important crops was wild rice, an aquatic grass whose long and lovely seeds had value for their "shelf life," flavour, abundance in certain places, and value as a trade good. Fall also found game mammals at the plumpest point in their seasonal cycle. The meat, stripped of its fat, was cut into thin strips and dried in the sun or over a slow, smokey fire. After rendering, the fat could be stored as a source of winter energy and physical enhancement. Bear grease added lustre to their hair of both sexes.

The first Europeans to explore the North Channel of Lake Huron, the Strait of Mackinac, and the St. Mary's River encountered the Ojibwa, the Ottawa, and the Potawatomi, three closely related groups whose ancestors had migrated into the Upper Lakes region from the east some four hundred years earlier.[14] Native peoples and early traders frequented St. Joseph Island, not only because it offered opportunities to fish, hunt, and gather seasonal fruits, but because of its strategic location, its attractiveness as a "rest stop" on journeys to and from points on the North Channel and Georgian Bay, the Strait of Mackinac, Sault Ste. Marie, and Lake Superior.

The Ojibwa first encountered French traders, explorers, and missionaries early in the seventeenth century. The French were pushing westward in search of furs and the Pacific Ocean, driven in part by the need to pre-empt the British, whose bases on James Bay and Hudson Bay attracted the fur gatherers of the vast continental interior. Contact, trade, and the European claim to a general suzerainty — symbolized on 4 June 1671 when Simon-François Daumont de Saint Lusson (an envoy from Jean Talon, intendant of New France) raised a cross in Sault Ste. Marie — began a new phase in Aboriginal life. The European presence fundamentally altered the economic, social, and political environments, and even, ultimately, the natural environment.

Contact generated change, which escalated rapidly after the French established a mission and fur trading interest at Sault Ste. Marie. This outpost of French political, economic, and religious influence promoted a congress of Aboriginal cultures and (sometimes clashing) interests at the Sault. Whereas the Ojibwa had previously shared the area with the Ottawa and Potawatomi, the French factor attracted the Huron, Dakota, Sac, Fox, Menominee, and Winnebago. Representatives of some fourteen nations witnessed Saint Lusson's elevation of cross and crown in 1671.[15] Inter-tribal and inter-racial marriage followed, as did a more varied ceremonial life, the product of the exchange of songs, dances, legends, and creation stories. While the Ojibwa continued their seasonal and territorial rounds as before, their role as suppliers of fur in a North Atlantic market economy worked some new and varied patterns into the fabrics of their lives. Though always semi-nomadic, they now entered upon a campaign of rather aggressive territorial expansion in order to compete more effectively in the altered economic environment. Goods such as guns and ammunition, metal pots and kettles, and even blankets modified somewhat the way the Ojibwa lived, hunted, and prepared and stored their food. Mobility — previously a product of ceremony or hunting, fishing, or gathering — became conditioned by the exigencies of the fur trade.

The canoe itself responded to the imperatives of the trade. After 1603, it was the indispensable vehicle for exploring the country and driving commerce. This forced an adaptation in the craft itself. At first canoes were relatively small, from eight to eighteen feet in length, but the need to carry heavier loads longer distances ultimately increased the vessels' length to thirty-six feet or more. This also created a new trade in rolled bark to supply the canoe manufactories established by the French. After the conquest of New France in 1763, the British victors discovered a Montreal warehouse containing hundreds of cords of birch bark, stored until required for the construction of large canoes.

The introduction of rival European interests into the Great Lakes basin sharpened already existing rivalries. The alliance among the French, Huron, and Algonquian nations tempted the Iroquois, allies of the English, to breach the line that blocked them from the fur resources of the Upper Lakes country. In 1649 the Iroquois destroyed the villages of Huronia in what is now the Midland area of Ontario. Their furious onslaught temporarily drove the Hurons and some of their Woodland neighbours north onto the islands of Georgian Bay, into the Green Bay country west of Lake Michigan, and to the western end of Lake Superior. Here they found themselves penned against the edges of territory claimed by the Sioux, a people whose warlike reputation at least equalled that of the Iroquois. By 1700, however, members of the northern alliance had driven the Iroquois back into their homeland south of Lake Ontario, and divided the large peninsula separating Lake Huron from Lakes Ontario and Erie among themselves.

Tracing the migration of Aboriginal people and the expansion of their territory in the seventeenth and eighteenth centuries is somewhat difficult, in part because contemporaries often misnamed the groups, or because movements might involve whole communities or only a few prominent traders and their families. Groups of Ojibwa moved north of the Lower Great Lakes. Others found sufficient incentive in their trade to expand their influence beyond their base on the St. Mary's River to the north and west of Lake Superior. There they assisted the French in preventing the flow of furs to British posts on Hudson Bay, although occasionally they engaged in that trade themselves. By the 1730s the Ojibwa had established themselves at Lake Nipigon and as far west as the Berens River, Manitoba. As the Ojibwa arrived, the Cree — who had dominated the territory between Hudson Bay and Lake Superior at contact — expanded west to work the fringes of the great plains. Archaeologists locate the Ojibwa's predominant sphere of influence around most of Lake Superior, traced counter-clockwise from Sault Ste. Marie to the Keweenaw Peninsula, the product of migrations and conquests that began in the 1690s, when the Ojibwa heartland had consisted of a sphere centred on the fishery at Sault Ste. Marie, with radii extending to the eastern end of Lake Superior and a small area on northern Lake Huron.[16]

When the British expelled the French from North America during the Seven Years' War (1756–1763), they inherited all the imperatives, possibilities, and problems present in the northern environment and the northern alliance. Ironically it was a series of enactments beginning with the Proclamation of 1763 and ending with the Quebec Act of 1774 that helped fuel the American revolt, whose promoters ultimately drove the British out of the old American territories and confined them to the region north of the Lakes. Now it was the British who had to confront, on the south, an enemy at least as aggressive and territorially ambitious as the Iroquois in their day. The Aboriginal members of the northern alliance had also to decide whether they would close ranks against the European tribes by forging a line with their erstwhile Aboriginal rivals along a north-south axis in the heart of the interior, or whether they would treat and trade with the British and American rivals in ways that more or less respected a line drawn from east to northwest through the middle of the Great Lakes basin.

In the process of working out the larger strategic implications of the American Revolution and engaging in the typical diplomatic exercises calculated to test the strength and determination both of rivals and of friends, the British negotiated Jay's Treaty in 1794. Its terms forced them to surrender control of the Strait of Mackinac to the United States, and find an alternative site to fortify nearby. It was this reversal of fortune that prompted the British, reluctantly, to build Fort St. Joseph. To that end, they purchased the island from the Ojibwa in 1798 for 1,200 pounds of trade goods and a yearly annuity of trade goods known as a gift exchange. The Ojibwa ensured that the agreement included their right to harvest the island's food supply, as well as to hold their religious ceremonies and bury their dead there.

Chapter I

Why British Authorities Built Fort St. Joseph

To understand why British authorities erected Fort St. Joseph in 1796 requires an understanding of European history of the period. From 1688 to 1815, Great Britain was almost continuously at war. The wars were not passionate ideological conflicts with the destructive force of Europe's Thirty Years War (1618–1648) or the two world wars of the twentieth century. Professional armies and navies fought battles, which had minimal impact upon the civilian population. The civilians paid taxes, and young men found careers in the army or the navy, voluntarily or involuntarily. Some who became sailors had the misfortune to be drinking at a seaside bar when the "press gang" kidnapped them and forced them to serve their country.

In most of these wars, the chief British adversary was France. France was the strongest power in Europe, with a powerful navy and an even more powerful army. Moreover, France was Great Britain's principal rival for ownership of

North America, and one of the rivals in the Caribbean. Ideology, while not passionate, was a factor. In 1685, King Louis XIV of France (1643–1715) ordered Huguenots (Protestants) living in France either to become Roman Catholics or to go into exile. That very year, England's first Roman Catholic monarch for more than a century, James II (1685–1688), inherited the throne. Fearing that what had happened to the Huguenots might happen to them, England's Protestant majority chased James into exile, and he went to France. Louis XIV offered political asylum and assistance to James for reasons both religious and practical. A Roman Catholic king, he thought, and particularly one who had regained his throne with Louis's help, would be friendlier to France than a Protestant king. Louis's support for James II led to a war between France and the government of England, controlled as it was by James II's adversaries, Protestant King William III (1689–1702, James's son-in-law) and Protestant Queen Mary II (1689–1694, James's daughter).

The successor to William III and Mary II was Queen Anne (1702–1714), Protestant sister of Mary II and daughter of James II. Louis XIV continued to support James II and, after his death in 1701, James's Roman Catholic son, James (half-brother to Mary II and Anne). Anne had several children but none who survived into adulthood, and in 1707 the Protestant establishment merged England (including Wales) and Scotland into one country, Great Britain. No longer would they continue as separate countries with a common monarch. The Protestant establishments of England and Scotland feared that the Scots might choose young James as their heir, and as far as they were concerned, a united Great Britain held fewer risks for Protestants than might an independent Scotland with a Roman Catholic ruler indebted to Louis XIV.[1]

Queen Anne's government fought the War of the Spanish Succession (1700–1713) to prevent France and Spain from coming together. The last of Spain's Habsburg kings, Charles II (1665–1700), died without heirs in 1700, and he left his throne to a grandson of Louis XIV, Philip of Anjou, who became Spanish King Philip V (1700–1746). The conflict lasted until 1713, when the belligerents negotiated the Treaty of Utrecht. Philip would keep the Spanish throne, but would renounce that of France. Spain ceded Gibraltar to Great Britain, while France recognized British sovereignty over Newfoundland, what today is mainland Nova Scotia, and those lands drained by rivers flowing into Hudson Bay and James Bay. Louis also agreed to drop his support for James II's Roman Catholic heirs.

Under the circumstances, it was understandable that the French governments of Louis XIV and his successor, Louis XV (1715–1774), wanted no further losses. To keep what they had, French authorities built a series of military outposts in North America, most notably Fort Louisbourg

Parks Canada has partially restored Fort Louisbourg on Cape Breton Island, in the process creating a significant tourist attraction. The restoration will remain incomplete so that archaeologists, historians, and other scholars may study the site without interference from possible twentieth-century misconceptions.
Photo by Graeme S. Mount, 1987

(on Cape Breton Island), Fort Beauséjour (just inside what is now New Brunswick, on a hill overlooking the Nova Scotian border), and Fort Michilimackinac. This last, operational without interruption from 1715 at the northern tip of the Lower Michigan peninsula, sits where Lakes Michigan and Huron meet.[2] French control of Michilimackinac guaranteed French control of the North American heartland — the Upper Great Lakes and the upper Mississippi valley — lands rich in furs. For almost half a century after the Treaty of Utrecht and despite two more rounds of Anglo-French warfare (1739–1741 and 1740–1748), the French managed to keep what they had.

Beauséjour, an eighteenth-century French fort captured by British forces during the Seven Years' War, today sits within sight of the Trans-Canada Highway south of Sackville, New Brunswick. *Photo by Graeme S. Mount, 1981*

Then came the Seven Years' War (1756–1763). This time the defeat Great Britain inflicted upon France was decisive. In 1759, British forces under General James Wolfe defeated French forces defending Quebec City at the Battle of the

Plains of Abraham. As part of the peace settlement, the Treaty of Paris negotiated in 1763, France renounced all territorial claims and ambitions on continental North America. She would retain her Caribbean islands as well as St. Pierre and Miquelon in the Gulf of St. Lawrence, but Great Britain would inherit the St. Lawrence and Mississippi valleys and France's North American forts, including Fort Michilimackinac. Spain would cede Florida to Great Britain.

An actor dressed as a soldier poses at Fort Michilimackinac. Fort Michilimackinac, a contemporary of Fort Beauséjour, was a centre for first French, then British soldiers and fur traders at the northern tip of the lower Michigan peninsula (where lakes Michigan and Huron meet). British authorities relocated the fort to Mackinac Island during the War of Independence and destroyed Fort Michilimackinac, but the State of Michigan has restored it as a tourist attraction.
Photo by Graeme S. Mount, 1988

37

British control of North America lasted less than a generation. Residents of the British colonies along the Atlantic seaboard, from New Hampshire to Georgia, no longer had reason to fear a French invasion. Conflicting territorial claims, like those of Virginia and New France in the valleys of the Ohio and Mississippi rivers, vanished with the Treaty of Paris. The colonists of British America could afford the luxury of a quarrel with their erstwhile protector, their own Mother Country.

There were several problems, most notably the questions of whether the colonists should help pay the costs of the Seven Years' War and the location of the boundary between Quebec and the New England colonies. However, an incident at Fort Michilimackinac also helped provoke the colonial rebellion. British and French diplomats had negotiated the transfer of French North America to British sovereignty. Those who inhabited the affected areas were not consulted. Some thought British officials more arrogant and less generous than their French counterparts had been, and there were well-substantiated fears that British colonists would soon occupy lands west of the Appalachians and displace the people who had lived there for thousands of years. Local politics became intertwined with European and trans-Atlantic diplomacy. Both colonists and indigenous people had reasons for directing anger at British authorities.

In the spring of 1763, an Ottawa chief named Pontiac led a rebellion that bears his name. Historian Robert S. Allen has attributed much of the responsibility for Pontiac's rebellion to insensitivity on the part of Sir William Johnson, British Superintendent of Indian Affairs. On 9 September 1761, Allen says, Johnson told a Detroit gathering

that he regarded the Wyandot as the leaders of the incipient Western Confederacy. This speech angered the influential Ottawa Confederacy (Ottawa,

Potawatomi, and Ojibwa) and further aggravated Indian restlessness. Johnson's comments, coupled with the fear of the irretrievable loss of their lands and culture, their anger at British austerity measures aimed partly at the redman, and misinformation that the French King was returning to help them, combined to goad the Indians under the leadership of the Ottawa Chief Pontiac into open rebellion ... in May of 1763.[3]

Minavana, chief of the Ojibwa (known as "Chippewa" in the United States) who lived near Fort Michilimackinac, managed to convince the fort's British commander, Captain George Etherington, that he was a friend. Such "friendship" led Etherington to reject warnings, including one from fur trader Alexander Henry, about plots to capture the fort. Minavana and his friends suggested that when the annual celebration of the birthday of King George III (1760–1820) took place early in June, activities should include a game of baggatiway (which resembled lacrosse) between the Chippewa and visiting Sauk. In the words of Michigan historian Bruce Catton:

Indian women clustered all around, wrapped in blankets, watching with stolid interest; British officers looked on, laughing, calling out to make bets on one side or the other. The tide of play surged up and down the field, and finally one player gave a mighty swipe with his racket and sent the ball flying into the fort. The players ran in after it, shouting and shouldering one another ... and then the Indian women drew tomahawks from under their blankets and handed them to the stripped-down braves, and all at once the idling British were mercilessly cut down.[4]

The area around Fort Michilimackinac where the baggatiway game of 1763, played to commemorate the birthday of George III, went out of control.
Photo by Andre Laferriere, 1998

Chippewas killed most of the people inside the fort, one exception being Alexander Henry. He managed to escape and write about his experience. Henry wrote:

> The dead were scalped and mangled; the dying were writhing and shrieking under the unsatiated knife and tomahawk; and from the bodies of some, ripped open, their butchers were drinking the blood.[5]

(Of course, there were several occasions in the history of North America where those who perpetrated a massacre were people of European descent. Viewers of Western films are well aware that no one had a monopoly on atrocities.)

In the aftermath of Pontiac's rebellion, the British government issued the Proclamation of 1763, which closed lands west of the Appalachians to colonial settlement. In 1768, Johnson negotiated the Treaty of Fort Stanwix with the Six Nations of the Iroquois Confederacy, whereby the Ohio

River would become the boundary between Aboriginals and those of European descent. The Iroquois abandoned land south of the Ohio in exchange for the commitment that they could keep their lands to its north.[6] This, however, was too generous as far as many British colonists were concerned. Some of them wanted those lands for themselves.

By 1775, rebellious colonists (by no means *everyone* who lived in the Thirteen Colonies) and British forces were fighting each other. On 4 July 1776, celebrated thereafter as the birthday of the United States, colonial leaders met at Philadelphia and issued a Declaration of Independence. Both Americans and British sought assistance from the First Nations.[7] Aware that hostile forces might capture Fort Michilimackinac, which they had managed to reoccupy after the massacre, the British destroyed it. Between 1779 and 1781, they relocated their army base on Mackinac Island, a few kilometres to the east on an island in Lake Huron.

Meanwhile, the government of the new French king, Louis XVI (1774–1792), intervened on the side of the American colonists, not out of love for them but out of conviction that a divided British Empire would be advantageous for France. Fortunately for the survival of a separate British North America (today's Canada), neither the French nor the Americans wanted to see the other in control of the St. Lawrence valley. Both allies preferred to see it remain in the hands of their British enemies. American forces occupied Montreal and approached Quebec City in 1775, months before the Declaration of Independence, when their war aims were not clear. The New England soldiers came from a part of the world where Puritans had long held French-Canadian Roman Catholics in contempt, and they treated French-Canadians, whom they professed to be liberating, with a minimum of deference and respect. An attack on the now-British citadel at Quebec City on New Year's Eve 1775 failed completely, and when spring returned and reinforcements arrived from Great Britain, the American occupiers retreated. General George Washington, the

American military commander, vetoed plans to have the Marquis de Lafayette sail up the St. Lawrence River out of fear that once there, the French would never leave. Washington was old enough to remember the days when British colonists lived in fear of a French invasion, and he wanted French troops to remain on the other side of the Atlantic. As for the French, they preferred a small, weak United States that would have to depend on France to a strong United States that dominated the entire North American continent.

By 1783, all parties were ready for peace, and their diplomats met in Paris. No party gained as much as it wanted, but the British were prepared to make generous concessions. They no longer had the political will to fight their own people, especially once they knew the cost of occupying the thirteen rebellious colonies. Richard Oswald, the chief British negotiator, was a businessman who did not consider questions of flags and sovereignty to be terribly important. For him, the issues were peace and commerce. Once peace was restored there would be commerce, and as Great Britain had the stronger economy, British merchants would earn fortunes trading with the United States. Dealing with Oswald were three American celebrities: John Adams, later the second president of the United States; Benjamin Franklin, a world-class writer and scientist; and John Jay, later Chief Justice of the Supreme Court of the United States.

Article II of the 1783 Treaty of Paris established the boundary between British North America and the United States. West of the point at which the 45th parallel intersects with the St. Lawrence (south of modern Cornwall, Ontario and north of Massena, New York), the boundary would be the St. Lawrence River, the Great Lakes, and connecting waterways. Lands north of the St. Mary's River, which connects Lake Superior with Lake Huron, would remain British. Lands to the south would become American.

Those terms, acceptable to Oswald and the government of Lord Shelburne in London, proved provocative, even incendiary. Throughout the War of Independence, the British had managed to retain all their inland forts — Niagara, Detroit, Mackinac — but in the 1783 Treaty of Paris, they agreed to surrender sovereignty and ownership of the lands on which they stood to the United States. Once again, those who lived on those lands were not consulted, notwithstanding Johnson's 1768 Treaty of Fort Stanwix. Sir Frederick Haldimand, Governor of Quebec, realized that many felt a strong sense of betrayal. Haldimand also was aware that, given the disparities in population between British North America and the United States, Great Britain needed assistance from those people.[8] There was no guarantee that the First Nations would be helpful, even friendly or benevolently neutral in any future Anglo-American conflict. They might well fight, or at the very least allow the defeat of, the party that had provoked Pontiac's rebellion in 1763 and ignored the Treaty of Fort Stanwix twenty years later. There might even have been another Pontiac-like rebellion, costly in terms of lives to Americans, British, and Natives.[9]

Of necessity, then, British authorities decided to maintain a presence in the Upper Great Lakes — at Forts Niagara, Detroit, and Mackinac — notwithstanding the Treaty of Paris. To have withdrawn would have meant a loss of credibility among Aboriginal peoples, and, probably, a forced British withdrawal from the rest of British North America within a generation or two. The highly decentralized Articles of Confederation, which in effect served as the United States' constitution until 1789, provided for such a weak central government that there was little difficulty in maintaining the forts. That weak government even provided a pretext for British failure to withdraw. American authorities failed to maintain their commitments under the 1783 treaty to compensate Loyalists — colonists who had sympathized with the British cause — for loss of property during the War of Independence, and if they could violate one article of the treaty, the British need not hasten to comply with another.

The French Revolution of 1789 led to changes that terminated the reign of Louis XVI in 1792. In January 1793, convicted of treason, Louis died on the guillotine. Almost at once, Great Britain went to war against revolutionary France. Yet another war with France convinced British authorities that they could not afford too many enemies and too many conflicts at once. They would have to placate the government of the United States, especially since a new constitution, negotiated in 1787 and implemented two years later, had given that country a more powerful central government.

George Washington, the first president of the United States (1789–1797), sent John Jay to London to settle outstanding issues, one of which was the ongoing occupation of the inland forts. On 19 November 1794 Jay and the British Secretary of State for Home Affairs, Lord Grenville, signed a formal treaty whereby the British promised to evacuate those forts by 1 June 1796. When they learned the news, the Indians were in no position to react. A general of the United States Army known as Mad Anthony Wayne had inflicted a decisive defeat upon them at the Battle of Fallen Timbers, 20 August 1794. Grenville and Jay were unaware of this development when they signed their agreement, but that it had happened forced the First Nations to accept the inevitable.[10] Lands awarded to the United States by the 1783 Treaty of Paris would become *de facto* as well as *de jure* United States territory, open to settlement by United States citizens.

In the aftermath of Jay's Treaty, British forces had to evacuate Fort Niagara, Fort Detroit, and Fort Mackinac — all of which happened to be on the wrong side of the border. Evacuate they did, but a total abandonment of the Great Lakes basin west of Lake Ontario would have sent inhabitants of the region the wrong message. These people already had reason enough to believe that the British had capitulated before the awesome power of the despicable Americans. If the government in London, Governor Sir Guy Carleton in Quebec City, and Lieutenant-Governor Sir John

Graves Simcoe of Upper Canada (carved from Quebec in 1791) wanted to preserve British North America, they had to offer some evidence of military strength and commitment. Without such, any hope of Indian support would be non-existent, and without Indian allies, British North America would be living on borrowed time. Accordingly, as British forces withdrew from Forts Niagara, Detroit, and Mackinac, they relocated on the Canadian side of the border. Fort George became the Canadian twin of Fort Niagara; the garrisons could easily see each other across the Niagara River. Fort Malden became the British counterpart of Fort Detroit, and Fort St. Joseph balanced Fort Mackinac.

Unlike Fort Niagara and Fort George, Fort Mackinac and Fort St. Joseph were not visible one from the other. Like Fort Mackinac, Fort St. Joseph was located on an island, St. Joseph Island — where the St. Mary's River flows into Lake Huron. Energetic canoeists could travel from Fort St. Joseph to Fort Mackinac within a few hours on a calm summer's day. St. Joseph Island was not the first choice of British authorities. They investigated a fort on the mainland at Thessalon, a few kilometres to the east, but navigational hazards proved decisive. Larger vessels could approach Fort St. Joseph more readily than the shoal-infested junction of the Thessalon River and Lake Huron.[11]

To have built the fort at the Canadian Sault Ste. Marie might have made good sense. After all, as of 1796 there was a civilian population already there.[12] However, a "Commission Report" of 9 September 1825, at which time a new location for a fort was under discussion, included an explanation:

Though the river is only forty-five miles [in length], there are so many rapids, shoals and rocks that vessels are frequently ten to fourteen days going that distance.

The author of those words failed to note the presence of Fort Brady on the American side of the St. Mary's River.[13]

A British Army engineer from Montreal, John Humphrey, described the advantages of St. Joseph Island to Simcoe:

[T]he Island of St. Joseph is in the direct route of the canoes from the French River, and on the north side the ship channel to St. Mary's, which passes through Lake George, the narrows leading into which are not more than 200 yards wide. A Battery at these narrows dependent on a Post at St. Joseph's would effectually command this communication; there is a channel for boats or canoes to the southward of the ship channel and which is generally made use of being the nearest, but they must even then pass within sight of the island of St. Joseph.[14]

Chapter II

Construction of Fort St. Joseph

Construction of Fort St. Joseph began in the summer of 1796. To authorities in Quebec (what is now Quebec City), St. Joseph Island was too remote for serious consideration. Gother Mann, the Commanding Officer of the Corps of Royal Engineers, had overlooked the transfer of troops from Mackinac Island to a location in British territory. Lord Dorchester, Governor of British North America, doubted the need for a fort in the Upper Great Lakes, but Sir John Graves Simcoe, Lieutenant-Governor of Upper Canada, insisted. Finally, in the spring of 1796, Lord Dorchester ordered the move. He had reluctantly concluded that a fort in northwesternmost Lake Huron was justifiable if it assisted in retaining the allegiance of the Aboriginals and in replacing Michilimackinac as the hub of the fur trade.[1]

After the rejection of Thessalon as a possible site (see Chapter 1), Lieutenant Andrew Foster and a small garrison arrived on St. Joseph Island to establish a temporary settlement and to select the best location for the future fort. From his command post in Quebec, in April 1797 Gother Mann recommended that the garrison begin construction of the blockhouse, kitchen, and bakehouse. By then, Captain Peter Drummond and his men had replaced Foster's group as the garrison at the fort. Fort St. Joseph's northerly location and the short construction season there forced those charged with building the fort to establish adequate accommodations for anyone unfortunate enough to be stationed there. Until completion of the blockhouse, the soldiers resided in temporary huts.[2]

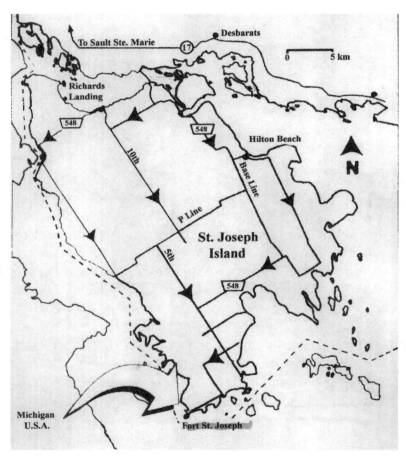

Lieutenant Andrew Foster and a small garrison chose the southern tip of St. Joseph Island as the ideal location for the new fort. Also shown on the map are the roads that have since been built on the island.
Courtesy of Parks Canada

The British leased but did not formally purchase the island before construction began. Colonel Alexander McKee, deputy superintendent of Indian Affairs, and Captain Thomas McKee, his son and superintendent of Fort St. Joseph, met with the local natives in the summer of 1797 to purchase the island. The parties reached a settlement, and in 1798, government ships reached Fort St. Joseph with three different officers from the Indian Department and the agreed payment. One observer described the scene of 13 June 1798:

Many types of trade copied earlier Indian ornaments made in other materials such as bark, leather, shell, or stone. For example, headbands and armbands were originally made from skins and hair pipes from shells before they were reproduced in silver. In this portrait by Paul Kane, an Ojibwa Indian wears clothes of European style, however, the series of crescent gorgets suspended from his neck, his silver wrist bands, and the leg bands serving as garters are distinctly Indian in inspiration. *Courtesy of the Museum, Sault Ste. Marie, Ontario*

These two Ottawa chiefs from Lake Huron have dressed in their finest clothing to meet with the representative of the British king. Their prestige is evident in the amount of silver they are wearing. While the fur trader saw the value of a piece of silver in simple monetary terms, the Indians attached to it other social values. *Courtesy of the Museum, Sault Ste. Marie, Ontario*

The whole of the Indian tribes to whom the goods were to be delivered, having assembled on the ground...; the merchandise, consisting of blankets, broad-cloths of every colour, guns, flints, powder, shots, ribbons, a few large silver medals for chiefs, steels for striking fire, some silver brooches, earrings and drops, and a very moderate quantity of rum, reduced to one third of the ordinary strength; the whole of these articles were worth, according to their value at Montreal, five thousand pounds.[3]

Lieutenant Thomas Lacey of the Royal Corps of Engineers and six skilled civilian construction workers had arrived in June 1797 and proceeded with construction of the blockhouse and kitchen. The very remoteness of the fort created difficulties in co-ordinating preparations to be completed by

In the exchange of gifts that took place at Indian-European ceremonial councils, the Indians received a variety of goods including clothing, weapons, and silver ornaments. These Huron leaders have posed in their finery for the painter Henry D. Thielcke. They are wearing an Indian adaptation of European military dress, heavily decorated with silver arm bands, gorgets, medals, and earrings. The textiles are of European manufacture as are the beads used for decoration on the moccasins and leggings. A number of the men in the foreground also sport French-Canadian style *ceinture flechée*.

For further information refer to George Irving Quimby's *Indian Culture and European Trade Goods*.

Drummond's men before Lacey's arrival. Drummond had received orders to begin construction at once, but the necessary tools remained at Amherstburg (near modern Windsor, Ontario). Even without them, Lacey and his men tried to do what they could. For the remainder of the season, work proceeded slowly on the blockhouse and the kitchen, so slowly that by autumn they were still not ready for use. Also that autumn, Drummond managed to erect a palisade around the temporary camp at La Pointe Point, where his crew would pass the winter. As the blockhouse at St. Joseph's Point remained far from finished, those remaining on St. Joseph Island had to use temporary lodging for the winter.

For their part, Lacey and the construction workers left the fort in November to return to Quebec, but Lacey's subordinates were not as fortunate. One of the soldiers described living conditions:

> My hut was about twenty feet square, formed of logs in the usual way, but had no chimney; this defect was remedied by a wide space paved in the middle for the fireplace, and a hole two feet square in the roof to let out the smoke — for there was no ceiling and no boarded floor — but it could boast one window with oiled paper, a tolerably good substitute for glass.[4]

Over the winter, those left on St. Joseph Island prepared square timbers and other building materials. Back in Quebec, Lieutenant Lacey formulated plans and prepared budget estimates for the following summer's work. Plans included construction of a wharf, a building for the storage of gunpowder, and a guardhouse. Lacey provided for a palisade at St. Joseph's Point, equipped with gun platforms, to guard the permanent fort.

Until 1798, the pace of construction had been relatively slow. With the arrival of Lieutenant George Landmann from Quebec, construction began in earnest. Only eighteen years of age, Landmann would supervise the construction of a "large block-house, [a] guard-house, a powder-magazine, a provision-store, and Indian department store-house, an Indian council house, and a baking-house, the whole to be enclosed by a palisade." He would also oversee construction of a wharf to handle shipping activity. Landmann travelled from Quebec City along the voyageur route — up the St. Lawrence River to Montreal, up the Ottawa River to its junction with the Mattawa River, across the short portage from Trout Lake at the head of the Mattawa River to the La

Vase Creek, down the La Vase Creek to Lake Nipissing, across Lake Nipissing to the French River, and down the French River to Lake Huron. Due to the length of the journey, he arrived later than he might have wished, with "no plans, sections, or even descriptions of the buildings" to work with.[5] Nevertheless, that summer there was significant progress on the blockhouse, guardhouse, kitchen, and bakehouse. Military plans called for four six-pound cannons to be sent from Amherstburg, along with the personnel to handle them, but they never materialized. Given the state of eighteenth century technology, the tremendous distance from Amherstburg, let alone Quebec, made construction of Fort St. Joseph a greater feat than construction of Fort George or Fort Malden. Again, with the arrival of fall, Landmann returned to Quebec, this time in a record eight days. There he prepared plans for the following summer's work.

Other problems arose due to haste. The builders of some structures, including the blockhouse, used green timber. Green timber, freshly cut wood not given adequate time to dry and cure, splits and shrinks as it dries, and it left the blockhouse walls too well ventilated. In summer, driving rain and ferocious mosquitoes would present problems. In winter, heavy snowfalls and driving winds rendered accommodations uncomfortable at best. The men tried to weatherproof the walls with clapboard. As the wharf faced into the prevailing winds, it too had to be reconstructed.

Because of the limited budget allocated for the fort, it was essential to keep construction costs to a minimum. In the summer of 1800 and without Landmann's guidance, Drummond continued to work on the enclosure, including the clapboarding of the blockhouse, and he managed to remain within budget.

Fire was an ever constant danger at Fort St. Joseph, especially as the winter (and hence the heating season) proved so much longer than at Fort George or Fort Malden. The smallest spark from the large stone chimneys could ignite buildings constructed with squared timbers or the

Professor Patrick Julig of Laurentian University and archaeological students dig at the site of the Indian village at the junction of the La Vase Creek and Lake Nipissing.
Photo by Laurentian University, 1998

Professor Ken Buchanan (standing) and archaeological students from Laurentian University at the site of the Indian village, which travellers to and from Fort St. Joseph would have passed at the junction of the La Vase Creek and Lake Nipissing.
Photo by Laurentian University, 1998

cedar shingles on their roofs. Fire gutted the bakehouse one evening in January 1802, and the blaze consumed all kitchen equipment and food. Clearly the fort required a new stone bakehouse remote from the other buildings. One year later, a fire smoldered undetected for several days beneath the hearth of the blockhouse. Another fire burned part of the blockhouse the following winter. The constant danger of fire required construction of a permanent magazine or storage site for gunpowder remote from the blockhouse, and built of fireproof stone and copper.

Reporting in 1802 on the condition of the military posts in Upper Canada, Captain Ralph Henry Bruyeres of the Royal Engineers commented that Fort St. Joseph's palisades and defences required more work. The palisade still lacked gun platforms. Bruyeres also recommended further work on weatherproofing and the replacement of wooden shingles by metal roofs. The fort's exposed position was precarious; without benefit of an inlet or other natural defences, the wharf would leave large ships vulnerable to attack. Under the circumstances, Bruyeres recommended that only small vessels use the wharf. For the moment at least, it would not be built for large vessels.[6]

By the summer of 1804, Fort St. Joseph had a new storehouse (10 metres by five metres by 2.5 metres), a workshop, two apartments, and an engineer's store. A newly arrived engineer, accompanied by skilled artisans, worked on the new bakehouse and a guardhouse, both of which were ready by 1805. The bakehouse had weather boarding and a new metal roof. The guardhouse had three solitary cells, known colloquially as "black holes." Yet, it appears that Fort St. Joseph remained, at best, rudimentary or primitive. Bruyeres thought that some of the buildings, including the kitchen and the powderhouse, should be replaced. The gun platforms remained unbuilt. Even wind could — and on one occasion did — topple the palisade. There were minor repairs in 1806 and 1810.

Fort St. Joseph Island remained on the periphery of the

British Empire. Its cannons and other armaments were ones that officers at Amherstburg, its source of supply, considered superfluous. As a result, they were few in number and low in quality.[7]

Despite its low status, Fort St. Joseph became more than a military post. As frequently happens around military bases, civilians flocked to the area for employment and erected their own buildings. Traders who followed the British from Mackinac Island in order to secure their trading privileges were among those who established residences and storehouses near Fort St. Joseph.[8]

In 1797, the first people to build outside the fort were Charles Langlade and another fur trader surnamed Culver. Other traders, associated with the North West Company, then built houses on St. Joseph Island. These included John Ogilvie, Robert Gillespie, David Mitchell, Jean Baptiste Pothier, one Mr. Chiset, and one Mr. Ferot. Others who built homes in 1798

The French River looking downstream, route of the voyageurs and the contemporary highway linking Quebec City, Montreal, and Lachine with Fort St. Joseph.
Photo by Michael J. Mulloy, 1998

included Thomas Duggan, a storekeeper; Guillaume La Mothe, the fort's Indian Department interpreter; Charles Langlade, Junior, La Mothe's successor; Charles Jean-Baptiste Chaboillez, from a family long connected with the North West Company.

There were several corporate residents. The firm of McTavish, Frobisher, and Company applied for lots on the neck of land to the north of the fort.[9] The North West Company had two large storehouses near the fort. The Mackinac Company, a consortium of traders from Mackinac, constructed two large storehouses by 1807. Given the remote location of Fort St. Joseph — hundreds of kilometres from Amherstburg, hundreds more from the provincial capital at York (Toronto) the headquarters of the North West Company at Lachine (on Montreal Island) and the seat of government (Quebec) — it is not surprising that amenities there remained basic.

Chapter III

International Relations, 1794–1812

Tensions along the international border were palpable. The diary of Elizabeth Simcoe, wife of Upper Canada's lieutenant-governor from 1791 to 1796, had several references to the possibility of war between the United States and British North America. On 7 August 1794, four months and twelve days *before* the signing of Jay's Treaty, she noted:

> We hear nothing but reports of war with the States; in that case I & the Children go immediately to Quebec, that place will of course be besieged but it is thought better for me to be in a strong place where hostilities will be carried on *regularly* than here [York] where constant depredations may be expected.[1]

If Mrs. Simcoe, with her privileged position was so worried, one can appreciate what less well-protected people must have felt. The environment along the Canada-US border then must have resembled what people feel along the India-Pakistan border at the turn of the millennium.

Most of the problems arose from trade. Throughout the eighteenth century, the world was divided into trading blocs. Tariffs encouraged British colonies to sell their goods to each other and to the mother country, and to purchase whatever they needed from sister colonies or from Great Britain herself. The Spanish, French, and Portuguese had similar arrangements within their empires. From 1636 to 1854, Japan was a closed country. Japanese subjects could not travel abroad, nor, with very few exceptions, could foreigners go there. Japan was not a factor in international trade. Even without these restrictions, trade between the eastern seaboard of the United States — where most Americans lived — and Asia would have been next to impossible. Ice blocked the Northwest Passage. At the bottom of South America, the Strait of Magellan and Cape Horn were among the world's most stormy and dangerous waters. The Suez and Panama canals lay in the future, and the route via the Cape of Good Hope took forever. This meant that once the United States had achieved its independence, it had few possible trading partners. Nor was the domestic market large: 3,929,214 according to the census of 1790; 5,308,483 in 1800; 7,239,881 in 1810; and of these, many were slaves without personal incomes. American merchants would have to grasp whatever opportunities came their way.

The renewed Anglo-French warfare, which lasted (apart from a brief truce in 1802–1803) from 1793 to 1814, offered such opportunities. The French Army needed food, clothing, and raw materials for its guns. The more French citizens there were in uniform, the fewer French citizens there were available to produce food, clothing, and other necessities. As long as France remained at war, the British Navy could sink French ships. Goods from the French islands of the Caribbean might or might not reach their destination. If

France represented opportunity to the Americans, the United States represented opportunity to the French.

British authorities understandably objected. Given the zeal of the French revolutionaries and the ambition of Napoleon Bonaparte, who became master of France in 1799, Great Britain faced its greatest danger of foreign invasion since the Spanish Armada of 1588, if not the Norman Conquest of 1066. Not until Hitler's proposed invasion of 1940 would there be another such threat. Because the French Army could not march without food or shoes, the British embargoed food and leather as strategic commodities and said that neutrals should not supply them to France or ports occupied by French forces. American and French authorities agreed that guns and gunpowder were strategic commodities, but they thought that the ban on food and clothing was excessive. American merchants insisted upon their "rights" as neutrals to trade with whom they pleased in what commodities, with a few exceptions, they pleased. They also jumped at the opportunity to transport cargoes between the French Caribbean and France. Aware that such shipments aboard vessels of US registry could not be sunk, the British invoked a precedent, the Rule of the War of 1756. That is, trade that was illegal in time of peace (such as shipments between the French Caribbean and France in vessels registered in the United States) remained illegal in time of war. For their part, US merchants and politicians argued that they had won their independence, and that the former mother country had no right to interfere with their activities. That the British Navy would stop American ships on the high seas and that British officers would then behave like customs officers and investigate the cargoes of the American ships was intolerable.

Arguments about contraband and the rights of neutrals were only part of the problem. British and American authorities could not agree as to what constituted a legal blockade. Under international law, a blockade to be legal must be effective. What did that mean? The British wanted to conserve their navy for sinking French ships. Consequently, they would put a minimum of ships along a lengthy coastline and declare the coastline blockaded. American merchants eager to sell their wares viewed such blockades "token" and ineffective and demanded the right to ignore them.

Impressment was an even more bitter issue. Until the second half of the nineteenth century, British law did not recognize the right of a British subject to renounce his British citizenship and become a citizen of another country. In other words, once an individual was British, that person was always British. The United States, by contrast, was a nation of immigrants that granted citizenship to people who renounced their previous citizenship. Thus it was possible to be British under British law and American under American law. Discipline was less severe aboard American ships than on British ones, and working conditions were better. Hence, some sailors deserted from the British Navy to work aboard ships of United States registry. When the British Navy stopped an American ship on the high seas, British officers frequently inspected the crew to see whether there were any British subjects. If they discovered any "deserters," they frequently removed and even punished them. That this would happen at all was offensive to American merchants and American pride. Worse, the British officers were not judges in an impartial court of law but self-appointed judges, juries, and executioners with an interest in increasing the size of their ships' crews.

Jay was supposed to deal with these issues when he went to Great Britain in 1794, but the British government was adamant. The British were willing to negotiate withdrawal from the interior forts, financial claims, and some boundary clarifications, but settlement of the maritime issues, they thought, threatened national security. Jay decided that half a loaf was better than none and negotiated a draft treaty that made progress with regard to the forts, the financial claims, and the boundary, but which left the maritime issues as they were. The United States

Senate agreed with Jay and gave its approval to the incomplete treaty.

For the next decade, American authorities had little choice but to live with what they considered to be a most unsatisfactory situation. The behaviour of revolutionary France was proving at least as threatening as that of Great Britain. First, there was the case of citizen Edmond Genêt, the top French diplomat in the United States. Genêt was so full of revolutionary fervour that he chose not to respect diplomatic norms. Nor did he respect American neutrality. Convinced of the righteousness of his cause, he used his position to hire pirates to attack British shipping as it approached the American coastline and terrorists to infiltrate New Orleans, Spanish territory. Spanish King Charles IV (1788–1808) was a cousin of the unfortunate Louis XVI, and his government sided with the enemies of revolutionary France. French forces could invade Spain and Spanish colonies overseas, and French ships could sink Spanish ones on the high seas, but it was intolerable to President George Washington (1789–1797) that Genêt could recruit terrorists inside the United States and orchestrate terrorist attacks from American soil upon the territory of a country (Spain) with which the United States was at peace. Washington's government declared Genêt *persona non grata*.

Other problems followed. The government of revolutionary France disliked both Jay's Treaty of 1794 and the Treaty of San Lorenzo, negotiated between the United States and Spain — another enemy of France — in 1795. (The Treaty of San Lorenzo established the boundary between Spanish Florida and the American state of Florida at the 31st parallel and settled American rights of navigation on the Mississippi River, the international boundary between the United States and Spanish America.) James Monroe, the highest ranking US diplomat in France, was supposed to defend the treaties negotiated by his government, but he joined in the attack. Washington then recalled Monroe and sent Charles Pinckney, brother of Thomas Pinckney who had negotiated the Treaty of San Lorenzo, to take his place. Pinckney's stay in France was brief and highly eventful. When he arrived, the French government warned him that unless he left immediately, he would be imprisoned. Pinckney fled across the border to Belgium.

Then there was the XYZ affair. Three sinister French officials, known only as Mr. X, Mr. Y, and Mr. Z, approached diplomats sent to Paris by Washington's successor as president, John Adams (1797–1801), and demanded bribes. Adams categorically refused to send anyone else to France without guarantees that the French would receive him with respect and dignity. An undeclared naval war between France and the fledgling United States Navy ensued. The United States was able to resist French pressures, but Charles IV's Spain could not.

Napoleon Bonaparte became French head-of-state in 1799, first as consul, then as consul-for-life (1802), then as Emperor (1804). He had visions of recreating a mighty French Empire in the Americas with the colony of Saint Domingue (modern Haiti) as its hub. In order to feed the sugar producers of Saint Domingue, he wanted territory in the temperate zone of North America. To that end he pressured Charles IV into selling "Louisiana" to France. Contemporary Louisiana included the port of New Orleans near the mouth of the Mississippi River and most of the land between the Mississippi and the Rocky Mountains. By then, Thomas Jefferson was president of the United States (1801–1809). Despite his francophile sympathies, Jefferson was alarmed. It was no cause for concern that Spain was the sovereign power west of the Mississippi. It honoured the Treaty of San Lorenzo, which granted the United States loading, unloading, shipping, and storage rights at New Orleans, and Spain was too weak to be a military threat to the United States. France disregarded the treaty provisions, and it had the most powerful army in Europe. Jefferson feared that unless the situation were to change, "We [Americans] must marry ourselves to the British fleet."[2]

Fortunately for Jefferson, the situation *did* change. Napoleon sent soldiers to crush a slave revolt in Saint Domingue. So many died of tropical disease even before reaching their destination that he aborted the enterprise, and when a US delegation approached to enquire about the purchase of New Orleans, he was willing to sell *all* Louisiana. By the end of 1803, United States sovereignty extended to the Rocky Mountains. Once again the United States could afford the luxury of a quarrel with Great Britain.

In 1805, ships commanded by British Admiral Horatio Nelson inflicted a decisive defeat upon the French Navy at the Battle of Trafalgar. For the next century, Great Britain would dominate the oceans. The British Navy became more imperious than ever. Definitions of legal blockade, contraband, impressment, and the rights of neutrals became more significant and — to Americans — more infuriating than ever. What remained of the French Navy also treated American shipping with contempt, but because of the navy's small size, French violations appeared less reprehensible to Americans than did British ones.

The most provocative of the British actions took place in June 1807, when the British naval ship *Leopard* visited the American naval base at Norfolk, Virginia. Some British sailors deserted while on shore leave and joined the United States Navy. Dressed in their new uniforms, they encountered their erstwhile officers on the streets of Norfolk and taunted them.

Captain S.P. Humphrey of the *Leopard* was furious. The *Leopard* set sail and waited in international waters just outside the three-mile territorial limit. When a ship of the United States Navy, the *Chesapeake*, approached, Captain Humphrey took action. The *Leopard* fired at the *Chesapeake* for ten minutes, killing three American sailors and injuring eighteen. The *Leopard* thereupon returned to England.[3]

The Jefferson administration could not ignore such an insult. Until 22 June 1807, British naval searches for deserters had taken place aboard commercial vessels, never aboard ships of the United States Navy. Worse, the *Leopard-Chesapeake* affair had taken place within sight of the United States coastline, close to one of the US Navy's largest naval bases. Jefferson had to take action, but, mindful of the War of Independence, he did not want war. He asked Congress to pass what became the Embargo Act. Like Arab rulers of the late twentieth century who withheld oil from friends of Israel, Jefferson believed that Great Britain and France desperately needed his country's merchandise. The Embargo Act banned the sale of American merchandise to Great Britain, France, or any countries or lands controlled by Great Britain or France until one or the other would mend its ways.

The legislation did not have the desired effect. Great Britain and France did not stop interfering with American ships on the Atlantic Ocean. The Embargo Act, however, created a first class depression inside the United States. The US economy depended on exports far more than the British and French economies depended upon American imports. Smuggling flourished in a manner without parallel until the Prohibition era of the 1920s. There were gun battles between American officers and smugglers on Lake Champlain, south of Montreal. American merchant ships claimed, despite the absence of strong wind, to have been blown into such British ports as Halifax, Nova Scotia, or Kingston, Jamaica. There their officers said that they needed to sell the merchandise in order to repair fictitious damage. The British could buy what they needed from British North America, and Montreal enjoyed unparalleled prosperity. Indeed, one joker suggested erecting a monument to the United States president in gratitude.

For its part, the *Montreal Gazette*, the establishment newspaper from British North America's largest metropolitan centre, regarded the Embargo Act with total contempt.

Mr. Jefferson ... put an end to internal taxes; for that suspension of commerce would annihilate the revenue....

It seems ... very apparent that the American republic cannot be considered a military nation, cannot be valued as a friend nor dreaded as an enemy, until it has a standing army with a permanent revenue for its support....[4]

Indeed, the *Montreal Gazette* appeared totally confident that British North America could cope with any challenge hurled from the United States:

Our government at home can easily snare us ten thousand veterans; the loyal and gallant militia in the lower province is forty-six thousand strong; and the militia of the upper province, principally composed of the descendants of Bruce and Wallace [mediaeval Scottish warriors], are equal to their own defence. We have at our command from ten to fifteen thousand Indian warriors, whose predatory excursions would keep the whole frontier, from the Missouri to Lake Champlain, in continual danger and alarm.

The scorn continued. On 17 August 1807, the *Montreal Gazette* said:

Although we have proved that the United States is not in a condition to injure England, we will for argument's sake admit all the exaggerated accounts of American power, with which her newspapers are continually filled. We will even suppose that the *hundred thousand militia* which the President has ordered to hold themselves in readiness are really organized, disciplined and equipped, and under the command of good officers, ready to abandon their farms and march withersoever the government may direct. The first question that presents itself is, What can this mighty army of militia accomplish? Can it prevent the British navy from searching for deserters and mutineers on the high seas; or save from contribution and destruction any city on the sea board? Can it save a single ship from capture and condemnation? Can it open a passage to any foreign market, for American produce; or convoy to the American shores a single article of merchandise which custom has made as necessary to the support and happiness of her citizens as the ordinary fruits of the earth? In short, can it save the nation from bankruptcy and ruin? The Northern merchants will lose their vessels and cargoes;...and the Southern planter must abandon the culture of cotton, rice and tobacco, and confine his agricultural operations to raising the corn, necessary to subsist his family and negroes [*sic*].[5]

Napoleon issued the Berlin and Milan Decrees, which threatened with seizure any ships of US registry that reached French-controlled territory after allowing the British Navy to inspect their contents. The British government countered with orders-in-council that threatened seizure of any French-bound American ships that did not stop for inspection. American shippers would have to choose which trading partner they preferred; they could not deal with both.

Congress and presidents Jefferson and James Madison (1809–1817) modified the Embargo Act, first through the Non-Intercourse Act, then through Macon's Bill Number Two, named for Representative Nathaniel Macon. Macon's Bill Number Two had a carrot-and-stick effect. It permitted trade with both Great Britain and France. If, however, Great Britain rescinded the orders-in-council while France continued to enforce the Berlin and Milan decrees, the United States would reimpose the embargo against France. Likewise, if Napoleon rescinded the Berlin and Milan Decrees while Britain maintained the orders-in-council, the US would reimpose the embargo against Great Britain. Napoleon said that he would rescind the Berlin and Milan Decrees but continued to act as though they were still in effect. The British government *did* eventually rescind the orders-in-council, but not quickly enough to prevent a US declaration of war. (It did not help that an Irish terrorist assassinated the British prime minister, Sir Spencer Perceval. Perceval's death delayed the decision-making process in London. The declaration of war took place 18 June; the British cabinet repealed the orders-in-council five days later, *before* it learned of the declaration of war. Given the state of early nineteenth-century technology, news of the British decision travelled slowly.)

In 1810, a contingent of impatient, angry young men — Felix Grundy, Henry Clay, John Calhoun — had won election to the House of Representatives. They called for action to redress American grievances against the British. A year and a day later, on 7 November 1811, General William Henry Harrison of the United States Army was "pacifying" Indians of Indiana. He fought and defeated them at the Battle of Tippecanoe, and when they fled, they left behind British-made weapons. The British Indian Department had distributed muskets as part of the formal gift exchanges that regularly took place between Indian Department officials and First Nations. While the Native people likely saw these muskets as a means of defending themselves from American aggression, Harrison's soldiers regarded them as offensive weapons for terrorizing Americans. American anger grew even more intense. On 1 June 1812, a beleaguered President Madison asked Congress for a declaration of war. For almost two decades, he and his predecessors had attempted to resolve outstanding grievances with the former mother country, and they had failed. Madison mentioned impressment, the British search of American ships, disagreement over the definition of legal blockade, and he hinted at the Battle of Tippecanoe:

> Our attention is necessarily drawn to the warfare just renewed by the savages, on one of our extensive frontiers; a warfare which is known to spare neither

age nor sex, and to be distinguished by features peculiarly shocking to humanity. It is difficult to account for the activity and combinations which have for some time been developing themselves among tribes in constant intercourse with British traders and garrisons, without connecting their hostility with that influence, and without recollecting the authenticated examples of such interpositions heretofore furnished by the officers and agents of that Government.[6]

Unfortunately, the calibre of British diplomat sent to the United States early in the nineteenth century left something to be desired, and British authorities were not as aware as they should have been of the extent of American anger. After all, by 1812, Napoleon's army stretched from Moscow in the east to Portugal on the Atlantic. It was not in the British interest to divert valuable soldiers to a peripheral campaign in North America when the imbalance of power in Europe threatened the British Isles. Yet, Washington was a new and undesirable place for a diplomatic appointment, and experienced, competent diplomats preferred assignments to Vienna or St. Petersburg. The United States was not a Great Power but a nation of bushwhackers and slaves. Washington was a raw, artificial community in the process of being carved out of the bush to serve as a capital city. Streets were unpaved, and in the era before air conditioning, its climate was excessively hot. Hence, the Foreign Office sent to Washington diplomats who could not be trusted with more serious assignments or junior people who might learn on the job.

Anthony Merry, whose personality did not coincide with his surname, found Americans totally uncouth. He was disgusted that when he went to present his credentials to President Jefferson at the Presidential Mansion (now the White House), Jefferson was wearing a pair of well-used bedroom slippers. When Merry and his enormous wife returned for an official dinner, they did not arrive to a fanfare of trumpets. To their horror, they had to stand along a wall until somebody yelled that the food was ready. As there were more guests than seats, they then had to race to the table to grab a couple while they were still available. Merry managed to shorten his stay in a city where he felt totally uncomfortable and out-of-place by pleading illness.

Merry's successor, David Erskine, was so young and inexperienced that he agreed to everything the American government asked of him. He had no authority to promise a settlement of outstanding maritime issues along the lines demanded by the United States government, and when he did just that, his British superiors in London overruled him. They repudiated his actions and recalled Erskine.

Erskine's successor was Frederick Jackson, nicknamed "Copenhagen." On a previous diplomatic assignment to the Danish capital, he had behaved so boorishly that even King George III (1760–1820) marvelled that the Danes "had not kicked him down the stairs."[7] Jackson accused the Americans of deliberately misleading Erskine and behaved so offensively that the American government demanded his recall. *Persona non grata*, he did not immediately return home but went instead on a public speaking tour of the United States where he voiced his negative opinions of President Madison and his policymakers. Once Jackson did return home, the British left his position vacant for a year. During that time (1810–1811), American anger at all things British intensified.

There is a good case to be made that there was no single cause for war in 1812. Apart from a few optimists like John Calhoun, who regarded it as a second War of Independence, or Henry Clay, who thought that the conquest of Canada would be but a matter of marching, it was a last resort. Madison and his predecessors had tried in vain to use peaceful means to protect American interests as they understood them to be. Successive British governments were understandably obsessed by the threat from France, both revolutionary and Napoleonic, and ignored what they considered the whims of Americans. Thus, the conflict began.[8] As the US Navy was no match for the British Navy, any fighting would necessarily have to take place within continental North America. Upper Canada — today's Ontario — was the most vulnerable target. Without Indian allies, its defence would have been hopeless.[9]

Happily for the British cause, there would be such allies, most notably Tecumseh. Tecumseh, a Shawnee who would die fighting for the British at the Battle of the Thames in 1813, had lost several relatives in battle: his father (1774), an older brother (1789), and another brother (1794). That he would join forces with the British enemy of his American enemy is quite understandable. In 1811, Tecumseh attempted to persuade Choctaw, Cherokee, Chickasaw, and Creek to join his Confederacy, and in 1812, he became a Brigadier-General in the British Army.[10] First Nations peoples irate over the loss of their lands would play a decisive role at Fort St. Joseph.

Chapter IV

Life at Fort St. Joseph

Fur traders, civil servants, and the military at Fort St. Joseph were always mindful that their outpost was the British mirror image of Fort Mackinac. It too was more than a military fort, for American fur traders organized the Mackinac Company, probably in 1784, the same year as the establishment of the North West Company. Some of the same people worked for both companies. As international tensions increased and the possibility of war loomed, political interference hampered the work of the Mackinac Company until, in 1811, its partners sold their assets to the American Fur Company, founded three years earlier by John Jacob Astor. Astor called the newly acquired company the South West Company (SWC), but its history was brief. Forced to suspend operations from 1812 to 1815, in 1816 it merged into the American Fur Company.[1]

The setting at Fort St. Joseph.
Photo by Michael J. Mulloy, 1989

Daily life on St. Joseph Island posed many challenges. The residents of the island included British soldiers, officials of the Indian Department, fur traders (many of them Métis), and their families. Isolation, scarce resources, and a severe climate profoundly affected everyone. One letter from Fort St. Joseph to Detroit mailed 8 February 1803 reached its destination, but the writer received his reply only 6 July.[2] The distance from Amherstburg, opposite Detroit (Fort St. Joseph's principal source of supply in peace time), was 322 miles (more than 500 kilometres). Mail to Montreal or Quebec City, some 1,500 miles or 2,500 kilometres from Fort St. Joseph, necessarily took longer.[3] Because of wind conditions on the Detroit and St. Clair rivers, not to mention those on Lake Huron, the trip from Amherstburg to Fort St. Joseph could take the best part of three months.[4] Also with regard to weather, Lieutenant Landmann arrived for the season 3 June 1800 in scorching heat. The next morning, six inches of snow covered the ground, and the troops wore overcoats, fur hats, and mittens as they celebrated the birthday of King George III.[5]

The military component of the fort comprised the main element of the community. The purpose of Fort St. Joseph was to protect the Upper Great Lakes from American intrusion, maintain a friendly alliance with the First Nations, and secure British control of the fur trade. To do this, the military first had to secure the island. From 1796 to 1812, no military personnel remained there for very long. Commanding officers and regiments were always rotating. This was routine at posts such as Fort George, Fort Malden, and Fort St. Joseph. The commanding officer was usually a captain or subaltern. Assisted by junior officers, he would be responsible for administration and the carrying out of orders from his superiors in York (Toronto) or Quebec City. The junior officers had responsibility for some administrative duties, along with discipline of the troops.

The regiments that served on St. Joseph Island varied in size. Lieutenant Andrew Foster and the 24th Regiment, who arrived in the spring of 1796, helped survey and clear land for the fort. That fall, Ensign Leonard Brown and twelve men from the Queen's Rangers replaced them, but only briefly. From spring 1799 until July 1801, Captain Peter Drummond, two junior officers, and forty-two men from the Royal Canadian Volunteers served at the site and assisted with clearing, preparation, and actual construction of the fort. Lieutenant Robert Cowell and a detachment of the Queen's Rangers served from 1801 until 1802, until Captain Alexander Clerk and men from the 49th Regiment assumed responsibility. By the time Captain Arthur Trew and the 41st Regiment had their tour of duty (1805–1808), major construction projects had ended and the fort was as developed as it was ever going to be. Command of the 41st Regiment changed four times: from Trew to Captain Adam Muir to Major Alexander Campbell to Captain William Derenzy. Between the summer of 1809 and the fall of 1811, first Captain Thomas Dawson and then Captain Thomas Ormsby Sherrard commanded a detachment of the 100th Regiment. Fort St. Joseph's most famous commander, Captain

Charles Roberts, took charge in September 1811. The 10th Royal Veterans under his command were the soldiers who attacked Fort Mackinac in 1812.[6]

Another military division represented at the fort was the Corp of Royal Engineers. Engineers would reside in temporary dwellings during the building season and supervise construction of the fort. Lieutenants Alexander Bryce and Theodore Depencier were the ones who surveyed the island in 1796 and selected the fort's actual location. Lieutenants Thomas Lacey and George Landmann also served tours of duty. Captain Gustavus Nicolls and master carpenter Wheeler Cornwall visited the fort to carry out repairs in 1804 and 1806 respectively.

The chimney at Fort St. Joseph, probably from one of the kitchens. *Photo by Michael J. Mulloy, 1989*

Life at this remote locale presented opportunities and challenges. British military regulations allowed six women and their families per company, and some commanding officers chose to have their wives and children accompany them. Few at Fort St. Joseph did, because of the harsh climate and isolation. Some feared for the safety of their families in such an environment. The commandant lived in relative luxury, usually in quarters situated in the blockhouse or a house provided by a fur trader outside the fortification. Servants maintained his household and prepared his meals. Some commandants would import livestock, produce, and other materials from Amherstburg and Montreal, while others tended vegetable gardens for them.

Junior or non-commissioned officers (NCOs), usually without wives, often lived in homes outside the fort, usually rented from an absentee fur trader. Others lived in modest quarters inside the fort.[7] More comfortable and spacious, the private homes offered greater privacy. The NCOs depended

The chimney and guard house at Fort St. Joseph.
Photo by Michael J. Mulloy, 1989

upon meals from the principal military kitchen, although hunting, fishing, and gardening offered opportunities for some variety.

Enlisted men resided in the barracks provided inside the fort, where conditions proved to be quite unpleasant. Living quarters in the blockhouse were cramped, and there was minimal heat during the winter. Because construction of the blockhouse had left much to be desired, protection against mosquitoes and rain was totally inadequate. On the other hand, the soldiers could enjoy some good meals. What came from the military kitchen was not very exciting, for a typical weekly military ration included four pounds of salt pork (packed years earlier in Great Britain), three pints of dried peas, six ounces of butter, six ounces of rice, and seven pounds of flour (for making bread).[8] Happily, however, each soldier had a parcel of land where he could grow vegetables, and there were opportunities for hunting rabbits, pheasants, and partridge. Northern pike, bass, trout, and the delectable whitefish supplemented what might otherwise have been a monotonous military diet.

Recent archaeology confirms that some who lived at Fort St. Joseph were able to enjoy at least one amenity of late eighteenth- and early nineteenth-century Europe — ceramics such as their peers, even their superiors, in contemporary Great Britain would have been using. Much of the chinaware was painted blue, most of it destined for use at the dinner table rather than for other purposes. The lack of variety in the patterns indicates a common, perhaps institutional, source.[9]

Desertion was a common problem in the British Army, and although civilian authorities could and did complicate the situation, British and American military commanders along the frontier managed to arrange a *modus vivendi*. Soldiers who crossed the international boundary without authorization would be returned to their units. In the absence of such an agreement, explained one commander at Fort George, retention would be next to impossible. The penalty for those who tried to desert could be vicious: two hundred to three hundred strokes of the cat-o'-nine-tails, administered so that other soldiers would watch and be aware of the consequences. Yet, desertions continued. Even as international tensions increased, a soldier's fear of his own officers could be greater than his fear or dislike of the enemy.[10]

At Fort St. Joseph, two unfortunate individuals, Private Keary and Private Patrick Myuagh, departed on 3 March 1809 to make their way to Fort Mackinac, about seventy kilometres across Lake Huron. In the early morning of 5 March, a search party found Myuagh frozen to death some fifty kilometres from Fort St. Joseph. In some respects, he was the more fortunate of the two. A sergeant, a civilian, and a native found Keary thirteen kilometres from Myuagh closer to Fort Mackinac, suffering from frostbite so severe that all his fingers and both his legs had to be amputated. The normal penalty for desertion was death, but in this case, nature had inflicted the punishment.[11]

In order to maintain an amicable relationship with the First Nations of the Upper Great Lakes region, the British government ensured that they received gifts from the Indian Department. At first the Indian Department had few resources on St. Joseph Island, only an interpreter and some supplies. Authorities quickly acknowledged this mistake and sent a storekeeper and a blacksmith. In 1796, Thomas McKee — son of Alexander — became superintendent of Fort St. Joseph, although he continued to reside in Amherstburg. The interpreter, storekeeper, and blacksmith remained on the island.

Historian Elizabeth Vincent has described the role of the Indian Department,

> whose primary responsibility was the securing of the loyalty of the which negotiated the cession of the Island, and organized the annual councils with their gift and information exchanges. While the agents were ostensibly independent of the military commander, the latter took a keen interest in their work — sometimes

to the point of interference. As the conflict with the United States approached, the friendship of the Indians became even more important. Their enmity would render the position of an isolated outpost such as Fort St. Joseph virtually untenable.[12]

In view of what *did* happen in 1812, it would appear that the Indian Department's representatives fulfilled their responsibilities very well.

In addition to providing gifts, officials of the Indian Department acted as intermediaries between natives and fur traders. Large gift-giving ceremonies or festivals would see the officials, natives, and fur traders exchange goods during the harvest season. Partnership with the First Nations, essential to the fur industry, also gave the British military allies against Americans who might invade. The role of the storekeeper was to maintain a warehouse and keep records of gifts from the British government. The store on St. Joseph Island contained such items as cloth, tobacco, knives, kettles, fish hooks, guns, ammunition, and foodstuffs. In exchange, the natives would provide furs, strings of wampum (small beads made of shells and used as ornaments or money), corn, pipes, and the highly sought after maple syrup. The blacksmith made tools and traps for the natives and repaired their weapons. The interpreter's task was to guarantee that natives and Europeans clearly understood each other, thereby keeping hostilities to a minimum. The Indian Department also provided the natives with medical services, including smallpox vaccinations.

In order to assist the fur trade, the Indian Department attempted to settle disputes among the Ojibwa, Ottawa, and Sioux, all of whom lived in the area. Such quarrels affected the flow of furs and threatened the safety of those at the fort, let alone more vulnerable fur traders remote from whatever protection the fort could provide.

At the same time, the Métis provided an essential service. They functioned as interpreters of language, and of the ways of the Aboriginals to the British and of the British to the Aboriginals. They also collected military intelligence about the strength and attitudes of the Western tribes in the years before the War of 1812. Without them, the fur trade would have been impossible, and the Indian Department could not have operated.

Some, but not all, of the officials at Fort St. Joseph were competent. The original storekeeper, Thomas Duggan, moved to Fort St. Joseph with the military from Fort Mackinac in 1796. As the blacksmith, surnamed Vasseur, wanted to remain where he was, Duggan recommended Louis Dufresne, who received the appointment. Dufresne, who did not live long after arrival, enjoyed an excellent reputation. Guillaume La Mothe, the interpreter at Mackinac, also moved to Fort St. Joseph, despite the fact that he and Duggan were incompatible. Indeed, Duggan asked for La Mothe's removal, but La Mothe remained at St. Joseph Island until his death in 1799. Duggan's addiction to alcohol, on the other hand, led to his court martial and dismissal in 1802, ostensibly for defrauding two Chippewa customers.[13] Charles Jean-Baptiste Chaboillez acted as interim interpreter, then was appointed storekeeper and clerk. Unfortunately, he had problems understanding English and could not maintain accurate accounting records.[14] In 1807, John Askin Junior, whose correspondence is one of the principal historical records of life at Fort St. Joseph, succeeded Chaboillez.

The ceremony of June 1798 to solidify the deal between the First Nations and the military regarding ownership of St. Joseph Island indicates the nature of the Indian Department's ceremonies. Lieutenant Landmann described the scene:

> The deed, on parchment, drawn up no doubt in the usual form, was produced and read by Mr. Prideau Selby, the Secretary to the Commissions, and interpreted to the Indians by Captain La Mott [*sic*], the interpreter.... Each of the chiefs of the various tribes

was required to execute the deed, which he did by drawing the animal of hieroglyphic representing his name and that of his tribe, and the officers comprising the garrison, including myself, signed as witnesses.[15]

As the ceremony continued, the festivities proved too much for some Upper Canadian visitors. Alcohol changed the demeanour of the natives and added to the excitement. Officials from the Indian Department believed themselves in jeopardy as the natives became more than boisterous:

After partaking of some refreshments of a very humble description, and the Indians having, on the other hand, heated themselves with the spirits,... we found it quite impossible to resist their forcing their company upon us, and although they in no way committed any acts that might be alarming to those habituated to their harmless familiarities, yet our visitors the commissioners began to view their position as dangerous and entertained some serious alarm for their personal safety.

Some of the first-rate Indian dancers came forward and gratified us with the Eagle dance, the Beaver dance, the War dance, and some other extraordinary feats requiring great muscular strength; the whole of them gala costume and painted in the most whimsical manner. Our commissioners, unused to being surrounded by six hundred or seven hundred savages, could no longer control their fears, and without much hypocrisy started off, and lost not a moment in securing themselves from these wild looking people.[16]

The commissioners clearly felt uncomfortable in the presence of the natives. Fort St. Joseph presented a strange and threatening world to those familiar with the relative comfort and safety of the more civilized outposts of Upper Canada.

Fort St. Joseph never enjoyed the services of a fully qualified medical doctor, and at least one of the paramedics was flawed in character and less than competent. A Scot named David Brown arrived at the turn of the century; Landmann described him as a having "very thick lips, always so disposed as to create a suspicion that he had just tasted of something very disagreeable."[17] Landmann also reported that Brown had a room in the blockhouse where he kept a

> six gallon cask of rum, which he asserted was of the finest quality, but of which no one, excepting himself, ever had any opportunity of judging.
>
> [Mr. Brown] ... contrived to be muddled by about two or three o'clock; and commonly retired to his sleeping corner by six, when he invariably commenced a severe quarrel with some invisible being, whom he loaded with every vulgar epithet in the English language. During a short time, these soliloquies afforded us amusement, for in the adjoining room, occupied by one of the subalterns, every word was distinctly heard.[18]

Brown provided a level of eighteenth century medical care that makes one quite happy to be living in the present. For example, Brown deemed a cancer spot on the lip of a Canadian carpenter untreatable, something that had to be removed along with the entire bottom lip:

Mr. Brown was a little fuddled, possibly he had taken one glass to keep out the fog and another to steady his hand. The instruments were soon exhibited, not perhaps in the best condition possible, which noticed, upon which the medical officer observed, "The edges are sharp, and that's the main point." He now ordered his patient to sit down on the only chair his room contained, and immediately on uncovering the cancered lip, Mr. Brown, to show he did not attach any importance to the amount of pain he might inflict on his patient, seized the parch of the lip which presented a deep hole for the edge half way down to the chin, and gave it a smart pinch and a twist at the same time.... Mr. Brown smiled ugly, and snatching up the knife, made one cut on each side of the cancer downwards to the full depth of the diseased part, and with a single cut horizontally took out the piece; then, with brutal exultation, shaking the piece of human flesh in the poor fellow's face, who had not uttered a single groan.[19]

Fortunately, according to Landmann, "It is worthy of notice that during the whole of that period [1796–1812] it was frequently mentioned with astonishment that not one serious accident had occurred to any of the government establishments, neither military or civil requiring surgical or medical attendance."[20] Fortunately too, Brown's tour of duty ended in 1801.

To many who had to go there, St. Joseph Island often appeared as a British Siberia. Stories of loneliness, boredom, and harsh weather were more widespread than any praise for the island. Even some who were inspired by the beauty sought an early escape from the post. When he arrived on the island 6 August 1801, Assistant Surgeon Robert Richardson — one of Mr. Brown's successors — commented that the place appeared better than its reputation. He liked his accommodation, and the food was abundant and tasty. Oxen, flour, corn, and fowls came from Montreal, and the natives delivered fish and ducks, and there were plenty of vegetables.[21] However, a mere six months later, isolation and cold weather had dampened Dr. Richardson's spirits:

I assure you we are heartily sick of this place. Our situation at Kingston was so very different ... that we feel the dreariness (and idleness on my part) much more severely.[22]

Obtaining supplies and goods posed some unusual problems, not the least of which was a system of trade that required a means of payment other than hard currency: alcohol became an all-too-frequent substitute for cash. Shipment of goods to St. Joseph Island required money, the absence of which obliged islanders to trade among themselves or with the natives.

John Askin Junior, son of the influential trader at Fort Mackinac and Fort St. Joseph and himself a Métis, was one of St. Joseph Island's civilian residents. His correspondence with his father details some of the problems of life on the island. Arriving there in the summer of 1807, Askin Junior referred to the "Coin of this Country call'd whiskey"[23] and said that if he had known better, he would have taken much more there with him. Fur traders bartered with the natives, exchanging rum and bread for partridges and fish.

When ships from either the government or the North West Company reached St. Joseph Island, the islanders celebrated. Shortly after the spring breakup, ships would leave Amherstburg with much-needed supplies. The long months of winter and the distance from the base of supply at Amherstburg created shortages. In a letter to his father, Askin Junior explained:

> I have no working Horse, Chairs to sit, Bedsteads, Cartwheels, Flour, Hogs, [and] slays [sleighs], tho[ugh] my store House is furnished with all of those things. I really wish that my B[lac]k mare may be sent in preference to the Packing Horse. She will be of service to me in Hawling [*sic*] Wood & answer extremely well as a breeding Mare.[24]

Clothing was a chronic problem. Summer uniforms were not available until half a century after the disappearance of Fort St. Joseph. The traditional red coats of the British military were unbearably warm in the summer, but far from adequate in winter. Captain Charles Roberts and his men faced the winter of 1811–1812 without overcoats. Those issued in 1807 had worn out, and in this instance at least, his superiors did not respond to correspondence from Roberts. On his own initiative, then, Roberts ordered thick blankets from Askin Junior. Women converted the blankets into coats, which lasted for two winters.[25] Without them, the men might have perished, and had they perished, events of the War of 1812 on the Upper Great Lakes would have been significantly different from what they were.

The community at the southern tip of St. Joseph Island was much more than a military post. Natives, Métis, fur traders, civil servants, and the British military and their families made it a thriving centre, at least by the standards of the era and region. However, its role as a military centre would have the greatest long-term impact.

Chapter V

The Glorious Moment —
The Clandestine Attack on Fort Mackinac[1]

In 1800, a British Army officer, Captain Alex Campbell, wrote a highly pessimistic report to the Duke of Kent, commander-in-chief of the British Army in British North America. The Campbell report dealt with the British Army's ability, or inability, to defend Upper Canada in the event of war with the United States, and Campbell regarded Fort St. Joseph as next to useless. It was "most injudiciously placed," he said. Its usual supply lines from Amherstburg would be non-viable as American guns could close the Detroit and St. Clair rivers to British military traffic. The alternative supply route — up the Ottawa and Mattawa Rivers, then across Lake Nipissing and down the French River — were infested with rapids. To send heavy reinforcements quickly would be next to impossible. If the soldiers at Fort St. Joseph *did* attempt any offensive action, thought Campbell, the Americans would notice whatever they did before it proceeded very far.

Nor did Campbell think highly of the British Army's indigenous allies. In his words:

> In 1800 the Post of St. Joseph was in a very open and imperfect state, the Garrison weakly manned, more capable of inspiring contempt than of giving the cunning and observing Indian a high Sense of our Strength and respectability; it must not be forgotten that gratitude is not among the Indian's virtues, if he has any.... To guard against an incursion of the Western Indians, four Companies at least ought to be stationed in that Post, the Works kept in thoro' repair, and no Indian, male or female, admitted within the Pickets.[2]

British authorities disregarded Campbell's advice, and it is well that they did. The policy, practised by successive garrisons, of establishing a partnership rather than an adversarial relationship with the natives produced formidable dividends on Mackinac Island in July 1812.

Campbell had good reason for pessimism. Fort St. Joseph was indeed militarily indefensible. Unless its garrison could launch a successive pre-emptive attack against Fort Mackinac, its soldiers were British hostages in a US-dominated environment. A windstorm of October 1811 toppled a stretch of rotting pickets. There was a shortage of platforms to support the artillery. Like much of the rest of the fort, the blockhouse remained a work-in-progress until 1811.[3]

Nor was Campbell alone in his pessimism. On 13 January 1812, one British Army strategist, A. Gray, reported to Governor-in-Chief Sir George Prevost that in the event of war, Fort St. Joseph would be utterly useless, commercially and militarily. There were more furs on the mainland than there could possibly be on an island, and a post on the St. Mary's River could threaten enemy traffic between Lakes Huron and Superior far more effectively than could Fort St. Joseph, located as it was on the open water.[4] Given these low expectations, the garrison at Fort St. Joseph performed a miracle in 1812.

Mackinac Island was familiar to the British Army. The British commander of Fort Michilimackinac, Lieutenant-Governor Patrick Sinclair (a captain in the British Army), first sailed into the harbour on the south shore in 1779. US Colonel George Rogers Clark had managed to capture British posts in Indiana and Illinois, and Sinclair decided that wooden Michilimackinac on the mainland was too vulnerable. Sailing to the island in a sloop, he became convinced that the hill where Fort Mackinac now stands was "respectable and convenient for a fort."[5] Construction of the limestone Fort Mackinac began on the island in 1780. The following year Ojibwa leader Kitchie Negon as well as leaders named Pouanas, Koupe, and Magousseihigan sold the island to the British Army for £5,000.[6]

Despite the boundary settlement of 1783, Mackinac Island — and its fort — remained in British hands until 1796, when the British withdrew in accord with Jay's Treaty.[7] Meanwhile, a cosmopolitan village of wooden cabins lined both sides of the street beneath the fort. Ottawa and Ojibwa, French-Canadians, Métis, British soldiers, and English, Scottish, and German-Jewish merchants lived there.

Article III of Jay's Treaty stated:

> It is agreed that it shall at all Times be free to His Majesty's Subjects, and to the citizens of the United Sates, and also to the Indians dwelling on either side of the said Boundary Line freely to pass and repass by Land, or Inland Navigation, into the respective Territories and Countries of the Two Parties on the Continent of America ... and to navigate all the Lakes, Rivers, and waters thereof, and freely to carry on trade and commerce with each other....

As the British had a head start, merchants connected with the Lachine-based North West Company had a decided advantage over their American competitors. One highly successful American fur trader was John Jacob Astor, who *did* establish a base on Mackinac Island, but even Astor had to buy furs from Canadian suppliers and then sell them to buyers in the United States or Europe. In 1811, Astor's American Fur Company and the Mackinac Company merged, with the result that Astor then controlled a significant portion of the trade in the Upper Great Lakes. At last, Mackinac Island became a centre for the fur trade. The outbreak of war in 1812 threatened to strangle Astor's infant commercial empire almost at birth.

President Madison asked Congress for a declaration of war 1 June 1812. The House of Representatives agreed 4 June, the Senate not until 17 June. The following day, Augustus J. Foster — Jackson's successor as head of the British legation in Washington — received official notice from the State Department that a state of war existed between Great Britain and the United States.

Major-General Sir Isaac Brock, chief administrator of Upper Canada since 1811, was a professional soldier in the British Army. Born in 1769 on Guernsey in the Channel Islands, Brock arrived in Upper Canada in 1802 and became a major-general in 1811. That same year Francis Gore, Upper Canada's lieutenant-governor, representative of the King, returned on temporary leave to England. Brock assumed Gore's duties on a provisional basis. As soon as he learned about the outbreak of war, Brock immediately despatched a courier to Captain Charles Roberts, commanding officer at Fort St. Joseph. Roberts received the message 8 July. Well aware of the importance of Fort St. Joseph, Brock had written several months earlier:

> Unless Detroit and Michilimackinac [Mackinac] be both in our possession at the commencement of hostilities, not only Amherstburg [near Windsor, Ontario] but most probably the whole country, must be evacuated as far as Kingston.[8]

Swift and efficient as Brock had been, Roberts was already aware of the outbreak of war. On 4 July 1812, an employee of John Jacob Astor's fur-trading company, Toussaint Pothier, had reached Fort St. Joseph with the news. Astor happened to be in Washington when war was declared, and his first thoughts were the safety of his property and possessions in Fort St. Joseph. On the assumption that he might do something to protect his furs and other trading commodities he had there, he sent messengers who could arrive before Roberts received official notification of the war. One of those messengers was Pothier, a loyal British subject, who told Roberts what was happening.

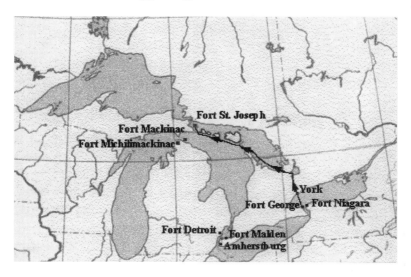

Route of British couriers to Fort St. Joseph, 1812.

Roberts thus knew that war had begun weeks before his American counterpart, Lieutenant Porter Hanks at Fort Mackinac, did. That advance notice proved critical, both to what followed immediately and to the subsequent course of the war in the interior of the continent. It was also a factor in the *status quo ante* peace settlement negotiated at Ghent to end the war. (Had the US Army performed well in the continental interior, there might have been greater pressure at the bargaining table for cession of Canadian land.) Since receiving his first commission in 1795, Roberts had served with the British Army in India and Ceylon (now Sri Lanka) before being transferred to the very different environment of Fort St. Joseph in 1811. An experienced soldier, he came from the family that would produce Lord Roberts, hero of the Boer War, almost one century later. He knew what to do with that knowledge.

President Madison's government was much more nonchalant than Brock. Overconfident, ill prepared for the conflict, and unaware of Brock's sharp mind, the War Department planned to notify the twenty-four-year-old Porter by regular mail. Historian J.A. Van Fleet accuses the War Department of "incredible negligence."[9]

Before the letter could arrive, Roberts notified Porter and his troops of the international situation, but he did so in a most direct way. The North West Company offered Roberts the use of the *Caledonia*, a seventy-ton armed schooner that it owned and that happened to be in the area. Roberts took guns and other supplies from Astor, and sought assistance from John Johnston, a British resident of the American Sault Ste. Marie. He persuaded some two hundred French-Canadian *voyageurs* from Fort St. Joseph and the Canadian Sault Ste. Marie to form a battalion, led by fur trader Lewis Crawford. He also requested reinforcements from Fort William, hundreds of kilometres to the west on the north shore of Lake Superior.

About four hundred Ottawa, Ojibwa, Menominee, and Winnebago warriors lent their assistance to Roberts' expedition of thirty-four privates, four corporals, two sergeants, an ensign, and two lieutenants of the 10th Royal Veteran Battalion, and of some two hundred French-Canadian fur traders (who constituted a militia). According to Michigan historian Willis Dunbar, some of those Indians had gone to Fort St. Joseph the previous winter to be ready for any war that might materialize. Whatever their ancestors had thought of the British at the time of Pontiac's rebellion in 1763, the Indians had long come to terms with the new reality. France was no longer a factor, and the British (most of whom lived on the other side of the Atlantic Ocean) threatened their way of life less than did the Americans. Elizabeth Vincent has suggested that some hoped that an alliance with the British might enable them to prevent American settlement of their lands.[10]

Two people — John Askin, Jr., and Robert Dickson — were highly effective in winning and maintaining Indian support for the British cause. Born in Michigan of a fur-trading father and an Ottawa mother, Askin, age 50, had spent the five years prior to the war as the senior British Indian Department official at Fort St. Joseph. Robert Dickson was a Scot who married a Sioux. In February 1812, as the international situation deteriorated, Brock inquired of Dickson as to the extent, if any, of assistance Great Britain might expect from the Indians in the event of war. Brock sent two Indian couriers in search of Dickson, and in June they found him in Wisconsin. Dickson said that he would find as many as he could and would accompany them to Fort St. Joseph by 10 June. He arrived that very day, accompanied by 130 Sioux, Winnebago, and Menominee warriors.[11] Askin estimated that he personally commanded 280 Indians in the siege of Mackinac, Dickson 113.[12]

Brock sent Roberts a second message ordering him not to act without further orders. The Indians were growing impatient, and it was with great relief that on 15 July, Roberts received a third message. This one told him "to do whatever he deemed necessary."[13] Later Roberts explained that he had had no choice but to act at once. Fort St. Joseph would have been "indefensible" if American forces had attacked *it*, and "the Indians who had been collected would soon have abandoned us" if he had delayed any offensive initiative.[14]

In the pre-dawn darkness of 16 July, Roberts' armada set sail. Hanks did not know that the British and their allies were coming. During daylight hours, the upper peninsula of what is now Michigan hid them. Soldiers at Fort Mackinac, high above the lake but on the southern side of the island, did not see them because Roberts and his men were approaching from the north, and hills blocked any view of the northern approaches. An exodus of Indians from Mackinac Island in the direction of Sault Ste. Marie had raised suspicions, especially when an Ottawa chief named See'gee'noe and others refused to say *why* they were heading there. Hanks asked a twenty-year veteran of the fur trade, a resident of Mackinac Island named Michael Dousman, to investigate. Dousman was also a captain in the Michigan militia. As Dousman frequently went to St. Joseph Island in connection with the fur trade, Hanks calculated that his presence would not raise any suspicions there.

This time, however, Dousman did not reach his destination. The invasion force captured him some twenty-five kilometres from Mackinac Island, but struck a deal. After all, Dousman and the people from Fort St. Joseph had known each other for years. If Dousman would promise not to tell Hanks and the fifty-seven men he commanded, he could have his freedom. He could use that freedom to warn civilians on Mackinac Island that if they gathered at the distillery, they would be safe. Dousman decided that duty and self-interest coincided, and he accepted the arrangement.

Dousman had learned that Captain Roberts intended to send a British trader named Oliver to warn the villagers. Dousman wondered whether they would believe a stranger and persuaded Roberts to let *him* be the one to go. Roberts agreed, but required Dousman to swear under oath that he would not inform Hanks and the fifty-seven men he commanded at the garrison, and Dousman was as good as his word. (Whether he should have been remains a contentious issue.) One hour before dawn, 17 July, Dousman began the task of waking and warning his friends and neighbours. Consequently, there were no civilian casualties.

Not every American captured at Mackinac was as honourable as Dousman. Captain Daniel Dobbins and his vessel, the *Salina*, were among those captured at Mackinac. Although Dobbins refused to take the oath of allegiance to George III, one of the British officers was a friend of his and said that Dobbins would be trustworthy. Accordingly, Dobbins received permission to sail for the British Fort Malden, opposite Detroit, and to take other prisoners-of-war with him. American troops captured the *Salina* near Detroit, and, contrary to the terms of his parole, Dobbins agreed to fight the British and their Indian allies.

Mackinac Island, site of the surprise British attack of 16–17 July 1812.
Photo of student assistant Andre Laferriere by Graeme Mount, 1998

Moreover, at least one American observer saw the role of Fort St. Joseph as less than civilized. The war had barely ended before William Puthuff of the Michilimackinac Agency wrote Lewis Cass, Governor of Michigan territory, warning him of the nest of vipers that the North Westers had for years nurtured, first on St. Joseph and then on Drummond

Andre Laferriere at Fort Mackinac.
Photo by Graeme Mount, 1998

Graeme Mount at the site of the 1814 battle of Mackinac Island.
Photo by Andre Laferriere, 1998

Modern Mackinac City, a tourist paradise.
Photo by Andre Laferriere, 1998

Island. Under the pretense of promoting commerce, charged Puthuff, these aggressive monopolists had prepared and sent out political operatives, holding British commissions, in the guise of small traders to cultivate the loyalty of American Indians. That strategy, combined with the distribution of presents on British-controlled islands on Lake Huron, had cost the United States dearly during the War of 1812. Puthuff's motives soon emerged:

> The importance of supplying the post of Michilimackinac with the means of counteracting the effects resulting from the aforementioned policy appears to be of the [utmost] necessity, and to effect this desirable object it will require the most active and vigilant attention of Government....
>
> [St. Joseph had been] the head Quarters of a vigorous, active, Enterprising, well informed and most Politick and designing company, who have

long and almost exclusively monopolized the trade of the North West.... [Its agents] were found to be our most active inviterite [*sic*] and most Enemies."[15]

When General William Hull surrendered Detroit the following month, Dobbins became a British prisoner for a second time. The penalty for violating parole was death, but another friendly British officer — this one at Fort Malden where Dobbins was being held — helped him to escape. He made his way to Washington and urged President Madison to promote naval warfare on the Great Lakes with the utmost vigour.[16] Dobbins may not have been as honourable as Dousman, but his patriotism is beyond question.

Roberts, his veterans, his civilians-turned-militia, and his Indian allies undertook a feat that would have challenged ironmen candidates for the Olympics. It was no mean feat to cross more than forty kilometres of Lake Huron, much of it in the dark, and this — plus the St. Mary's River portion of the trip (of equivalent length) — they did in twenty-one hours. At 3 a.m. the following day, 17 July, they landed on the northwest coast of Mackinac Island, almost diagonally opposite the fort. A march of about six kilometres across the island with their equipment and guns was the next challenge, and this they accomplished in a few hours. The *voyageurs*, accustomed as they were to portages, were capable of transporting artillery.[17] When they reached Fort Mackinac after some twenty-four hours of stress and exertion, they did not know whether they would face an immediate battle.

When Hanks and his men awoke, they quickly sensed that something was wrong. The town was so quiet that Hanks sent Lieutenant Archibald Darragh to investigate. Darragh found the villagers at the distillery and prepared to return to the fort. British guards would have taken him prisoner except that he took a pistol in each hand and walked backward. At the same time Fort Mackinac's surgeon, Dr. Sylvester Day, rushed from the village to the fort with news of what was happening. Day and Darragh could not compensate for the advantage that British forces already enjoyed, and Roberts issued Hanks an ultimatum:

> I summon you to an unconditional surrender of the island ... in order to save the effusion of blood.[18]

Fortunately, Lieutenant Hanks quickly decided that the 650 invaders were more than a match for his fifty-seven professionals, and he surrendered the fort without a fight. Three civilians, who had taken shelter at the distillery, advised Hanks that resistance would be useless and dangerous as the British had all the equipment they needed to take the fort, including ladders and ropes. (As though the discrepancy in numbers was not sufficient, they exaggerated British strength.)

In exchange for their surrender, most of Hanks's troops received permission to go to Detroit on condition that they would not participate in further military actions until US and British authorities finalized some permanent arrangement for prisoners of war. Despite Hanks' protests, Roberts charged three of Hanks's soldiers with desertion, but he treated them leniently. Two of them served as musicians for the duration of the war. Twenty other of Hanks's soldiers were British subjects, and they agreed to serve as soldiers under the command of Roberts. US civilians had a month to decide whether to take an oath of allegiance to King George III or to move to what was left of the United States. Michael Dousman had permission to remain neutral, but his brothers and four other men who refused to take the oath went to Detroit with the soldiers. Other residents of Mackinac Island wanted to stay there and took the oath of allegiance.

Hanks has received criticism for surrendering without even token resistance, but historian J.A. Van Fleet and Askin, who was actually there as a participant, have suggested that his action may well have presented a massacre. One shot might well have prompted the Indians to use their "scalping knives," said Van Fleet. Askin reported:

It was a fortunate circumstance that the fort capitulated without firing a single gun, for had they done so, I firmly believe not a soul of them would have been saved. My son, Charles Langlade, Augustin Nolin, and Michelle Cadotte have rendered us great service in keeping the Indians in order and executing from time to time such commands as were delivered to me by the commanding officer. I never saw so determined a set of people as the Chippewas and Ottawas were.[19]

Hanks may be criticized for negligence, wrote Van Fleet. Surrounded as he was by British territory and hostile tribes, Hanks should have organized better intelligence. However, he was wise not to compound his negligence with rash behaviour.[20]

Hanks explained his actions to General William Hull, his commanding officer. On 16 July, he said, an Indian interpreter had advised him

that the several nations of Indians then at St. Joseph (a British garrison, distant about forty miles [sixty kilometres]) intended to make an immediate attack on Michilimackinac.[21]

Hanks at once summoned a meeting of civilian adult males on the island, and the assembly considered it wise to despatch "Captain Michael Dousman of the militia" to see what was happening. Hanks reviewed the Dousman story — his departure at sunset, his capture by the British, his deal, and the element of surprise. So confident was he that his decision to surrender the fort was correct that Hanks requested "that a Court of Inquiry may be ordered to investigate all the facts connected with it."[22]

In the aftermath of his success, Roberts distributed prize money valued at ten thousand pounds among the militia and soldiers and gave weapons and merchandise to the

Indians. Aware that the US Army would probably attempt to regain what they had lost, the British occupiers then erected a second fort, which they called Fort George, atop Mackinac Island's highest hill. Once they regained the island at the end of hostilities, the Americans renamed it Fort Holmes, in honour of a fallen American major.

Roberts and his men were right. In 1814, Colonel George Croghan, US commander at Detroit, and his superior, General William Henry Harrison, attempted to retake Mackinac.[23] This was part of a two-pronged offensive against Prairie du Chien (on the Mississippi River) as well as Mackinac, the aim of which was to establish American hegemony in the Upper Great Lakes. At Prairie du Chien the Americans were successful, and their success increased the strategic importance of Fort Mackinac.[24] Without it, the British would have no presence in the continental interior. An American expedition set sail 3 July, reached Lake Huron nine days later, and then floundered. Nobody was familiar with the waters or the geography of northern Lake Huron, and there was incessant fog. There was a debate as to whether the first action on arrival should be to capture Fort Mackinac or to destroy Fort St. Joseph. Because the garrison from Fort St. Joseph remained at Mackinac Island, Fort St. Joseph lay vulnerable. However, news of an attack on the fort would probably reach the British commander at Mackinac, who could then summon his Indian allies to assist him. A surprise attack on Mackinac Island might succeed, while a delayed attack might not. The decision was to attack the easier target, Fort St. Joseph, first.

Accordingly, the American attackers reached Fort St. Joseph 20 July and burned it, but they did not destroy the civilian buildings, including the storehouses of the North West Company. The fact that Astor had buildings adjacent to Fort St. Joseph may explain their willingness to leave so much intact, because Croghan and his men were certainly willing to destroy civilian property in the Canadian Sault Ste. Marie.[25] Certainly there is evidence that Astor had strong connections in Washington.[26] Six days later they reached Mackinac, where the British commander, Colonel M'Donall, had learned of their presence in the region and ordered reinforcement of Mackinac Island's defences. Van Fleet reports, in language that today would not be politically correct:

> Every thing had been put in the most perfect order; weak points in the fortifications had been strengthened, and such aid as the country afforded had been summoned to his assistance.... More efficient auxiliaries could not have been found than those very savages who, during that brief period of delay, had gathered in large numbers upon the island. Batteries had been planted at various places on the heights which best commanded the approaches to the island. One was situated on the height overlooking the old distillery, another upon the high point just west of the fort, and others along the ridge back of the present town from the fort to Robinson's Folly. Thus that officer, though he had but few men comparatively in command and must have surrendered at once had an immediate attack been made upon him, was able, with the advantage he had now gained, to withstand a strong force.[27]

In other words, even as it lay deserted and vulnerable, Fort St. Joseph played a useful role in determining the course of the war and the shape of the peace settlement. It had diverted Croghan's troops long enough to allow the British Army to strengthen Mackinac's defences and to recruit Indian allies. The American invasion force did land, close to the spot where British forces had landed in 1812, but the British were ready for them. One kilometre inland a fierce battle took place, which the British won. Britain's Indian allies burst from the woods where they were hiding and killed Major Arthur Holmes, arsonist of Fort St. Joseph and the Canadian Sault Ste. Marie. The National Society of the

US Daughters of 1812 erected a plaque to Holmes and unknown American soldiers who died at the 1814 Battle of Mackinac Island.

Historian George Sheppard minimizes the importance of the militia and Great Britain's Indian allies to the war effort. Both lacked enthusiasm for the cause, he says, and Great Britain succeeded as well as she did because of British soldiers from the regular army.[28] That was undoubtedly the case on the Niagara Frontier, where Sheppard's study is concentrated, but it definitely was not the case at Fort Mackinac. There the two regular armies were fairly evenly matched. At Mackinac, the militia, the Métis, and the Indians made the difference. However, the Sheppard thesis stands nonetheless. To Roberts' dismay, the militia evaporated, anxious to return to the fur trade. By the time the reinforcements from Fort William reached Mackinac Island, the fighting had ended, and they too left for civilian pursuits. More than twice as many Indians landed on Mackinac Island after its capture as before, reportedly "to share in the rewards of victory." Finding sufficient food for so many people was a challenge. Roberts wanted to send them to Detroit where a battle was pending, but most insisted upon returning to their homes, and a few remained on Mackinac Island where they could enjoy the lifestyle. On August 12, an appeal for Indians to join the attack on Detroit arrived, but Askin said that they "were as drunk as Ten Thousand Devils." Roberts did persuade two hundred to go to Detroit, but they arrived after the battle had ended.[29]

That said, it is only fair to note the role of Jean Baptiste Assiginach, a.k.a. Blackbird, an Ojibwa who assisted in the capture of Fort Mackinac. Assiginach later participated in the successful British campaign at Prairie du Chien in 1814. When the British Army moved to Drummond Island, he went there too as employee of the British military's Indian Department. The fact that he could speak English, French, and several indigenous languages rendered him an ideal interpreter. When the army, including the Indian Department, moved from Drummond Island to Penetanguishene in 1828, Assiginach continued to serve as an interpreter. Highly religious, he also served as a lay preacher while at Penetanguishene. Upon retirement in 1849, Assiginach moved to Manitoulin Island and participated in treaty negotiations between the Ojibwa and the Canadian government.[30] Obviously, the Indian warriors at Mackinac Island did include a man of good character and strong convictions.

It would be unwise to exaggerate the importance of this British success. Yes, control of Mackinac Island — especially when combined with the British capture of Detroit one month to the day later on 16 August 1812 — gave British soldiers and fur traders undisputed control of lakes Huron, Michigan, and Superior — at least up to a point. Maintaining contact between British-occupied Fort Mackinac and British North America was in itself a rather formidable challenge. In 1813, the US Navy won the Battle of Lake Erie, and in 1814, the schooner *Nancy* perished in battle in Georgian Bay. Built in 1789 when Detroit was still a British outpost, the *Nancy* became the property of the North West Company about a decade later. Until the outbreak of war in 1812, the *Nancy* ferried supplies from Lake Erie, above Niagara Falls (the Welland Canal dates from 1829) to Sault Ste. Marie, Fort St. Joseph, and other places in the Upper Great Lakes.

The British military requisitioned the *Nancy* at the outbreak of war. For the next two years, she carried troops and cargoes of gunpowder, blankets, tools, and rum to Mackinac Island and other places of military significance. American sailors came close to capturing her during the 1813 Battle of Lake Erie, but she escaped in time and managed to carry vital supplies to Fort Mackinac. In the August 1814, they managed to set her alight as she was carrying supplies to Mackinac Island.[31] Mackinac Island *did* remain British for the duration of the war, but without undisputed naval control of the Upper Great Lakes, the supply lines were precarious. If the supply lines were precarious, British retention of the island was also precarious.

Nevertheless, Fort Mackinac resembled the cork in three bottles united at the neck. Defence was easier than offence, and when an American expedition led by Colonel George Croghan landed on Mackinac Island in 1814, the defenders resisted them and kept the island in British hands. Control of Fort Mackinac and lakes Huron, Michigan, and Superior must have been encouraging to the British and demoralizing to the US war effort. It was a factor in keeping the international boundary where it was — not farther north.

On the other hand, 1812 was a turning point in the Napoleonic Wars. Napoleon's army invaded Russia, and whatever threat remained to British security after the Battle of Trafalgar disappeared. On 14 September, Napoleon and his forces occupied Moscow, but most of the people who lived there had left, and the next day a giant conflagration rendered the occupation unfeasible. Once Czar Alexander I (1801–1825) rejected Napoleon's offer of a truce, the French Army had no option but to retreat. The retreat began 19 October, and a combination of cold weather, hunger, and enemy attack effectively destroyed Napoleon's capacity for war. On 31 March 1814, Allied armies entered Paris, and on 6 April Napoleon abdicated in favour of his son. Five days later, after the Allies rejected the idea of his son succeeding him, Napoleon abdicated unconditionally. Given that the victors did not foresee Napoleon's 1815 escape from Elba, his place of exile in the Mediterranean, Great Britain was free to concentrate her military force against the United States.

Thus, almost the entire War of 1812 took place as Napoleon's empire was collapsing. Arguably, the US position might have been stronger had it occurred at an earlier date. Yet, even that is not certain. Madison, like Jefferson, was a Democratic-Republican, not a Federalist like presidents George Washington and John Adams. Many of President Madison's Federalist opponents disapproved of the war and refused to co-operate. New England was a

Federalist stronghold. The *Montreal Gazette* quoted an anonymous New Englander as saying that the declaration of war ought to have been called "An act declaring war against the commerce and prosperity of the Northern States, and requiring the assistance of the British navy to execute it."[32] The *Boston Sentinel* editorialized:

> It is no longer doubtful that the Eastern States are invincibly opposed to war, and that nothing short of a conscription will fill an army for the foolish crusade. It is not less evident that our people will sooner become volunteers to drive from power the men who shall plunge them into a ruinous war, than conscripts to carry it on.[33]

If New Englanders had demonstrated greater support for the war effort, it might well have been possible for US forces to invade the St. Lawrence valley, as they had in 1775, and to throttle the one viable British traffic artery. As it was, they could only nibble away at the branches upstream, and even there, there was a lack of commitment. When the New York militia attacked Queenston Heights 13 October 1812, other militiamen felt no obligation, legal or moral, to cross the Niagara River and set foot on British territory. From the safety of New York State, they watched as Brock and his army defeated the American invaders. In 1813, General William Henry Harrison had limited capacity for offensive action because his Kentucky militia wanted to return home in time for the annual harvest. Attempts to march on Montreal in 1813 failed completely. French-Canadian defenders fought much more vigorously than the invading Americans and stopped the US Army near Chateauguay, before it could reach the St. Lawrence River.

The War of 1812 had been by no means one-sided. Despite British victories at Fort Mackinac, Queenston Heights, and even Detroit — which Brock had managed to capture in 1812 — the Americans won significant victories in 1813. The

Battle of Lake Erie obliged the British to depend, as had French fur traders before 1759, upon the Ottawa River-Mattawa River-Lake Nipissing-French River supply line, with all its rapids and portages. The British had to abandon Detroit.[34] In 1813, American forces burned York (now Toronto), capital of Upper Canada, and Newark (now Niagara-on-the-Lake). In retaliation, the British burned Buffalo and Washington, but this was of limited comfort to residents of York and Newark. Although Major Croghan's soldiers failed to retake Mackinac Island in 1814, they *did* burn the abandoned Fort St. Joseph and inflict property damage upon the Canadian Sault Ste. Marie. Significantly, stores of the South West Company, located east of the fort, escaped destruction — no doubt due to the influence of Ramsay Crooks, who was attached to the flotilla to safeguard the interests of John Jacob Astor. By coincidence, they found the North West Company's schooner, the *Mink*, offshore, downbound from Lake Superior, and captured her.

Crooks himself testified laconically of the occasion:

> On entering Lake Huron we shaped our course for Machedash, but this part of the navigation being imperfectly known, the commodore was after sometime spent in fruitless search of the Bay induced to steer for St. Joseph's. There the Schooner *Mink*, belonging to the North West Company, laden with Two Hundred and thirty Barrels of Flour for St. Mary's [Sault Ste. Marie], was captured and the Fort and Store Houses reduced to ashes.[35]

With the *Mink*'s capture came news of her sister ship, the *Perseverance*, waiting above the rapids of the St. Mary's River, ready to set sail for Fort William. The two American officers in charge, Lieutenant Turner and Major Arthur Holmes, sought to ascend the river, capture the vessel, and bring her down the rapids to Lake Huron. Warned by Indians, residents of the Canadian Sault Ste. Marie burned the *Perseverance* (so that she could not fall into enemy hands) before fleeing into the bush. While the Americans were able to put out the fire, they failed to sink the vessel. However, they destroyed the North West Company's buildings at the Sault and confiscated some of John Johnston's effects.

Destruction at Fort St. Joseph and the Canadian Sault Ste. Marie had no impact on the outcome of the war. Given the relocation to Mackinac Island of the garrison and its equipment, an aide to Sir George Prevost wrote: "St. Joseph in its present state Cannot be of any importance."[36] In 1814, after Napoleon's defeat, British forces transferred from the European front moved toward Plattsburg, New York, south of Montreal, but again, their impact was minimal. Although his forces were battle-experienced and more numerous than Plattsburg's American defenders, Prevost hesitated to attack. Moreover, most residents of Upper Canada lived close to the international border, on the St. Lawrence or Niagara Rivers, and were more interested in peace than in victory. Most British subjects — the people who would finance the war effort and supply the troops — lived thousands of kilometres from the war zone on the other side of the Atlantic Ocean. War weary after more than a generation of conflict with France, they were not in the mood to continue an unnecessary fight.

Even on Mackinac Island there were problems. Roberts did not trust his Indian allies and appealed for reinforcements of British soldiers, who did not arrive. He sent an officer and six men of the ranks back to Fort St. Joseph to protect it. The eighteen Americans whom he had forcibly enlisted proved so unreliable that they were more trouble than they were worth. Among the remaining forty regular British forces, indiscipline and insubordination were problems. Despite harsh punishments, they did not conform to expectations. In mid-August, one month after the capture of Mackinac, Roberts wrote: "One of them is now in Irons for striking an Officer in the execution of his duty."[37] Subsequent attempts to recruit Indians failed, although Roberts did manage to persuade some fifty *voyageurs* to form a militia. However, these people appeared totally unprofessional. British victories in Detroit, which surrendered to the British 16 August, and an Indian massacre of the American garrison at Fort Dearborn, Chicago, allowed British control of Mackinac Island to continue, notwithstanding the state of its garrison.[38]

In September 1813, Captain Richard Bullock of the 41st Regiment succeeded Roberts as commander at Mackinac. Askin thought that he was totally incompetent.[39] Whether or not Askin's assessment was accurate, the Americans under Croghan and Holmes — as noted above — made their share of errors, thus enabling Bullock to score a by-no-means-inevitable battlefield success.

On Christmas Eve, 1814, British and American negotiators signed the Treaty of Ghent, restoring pre-war conditions as much as possible. As Mackinac Island had been US territory when war was declared, it would once again become US territory. British forces would have to withdraw. One member of the British House of Commons, Hart Davis, said in support of the peace policy of Lord Liverpool's Conservative government (1812–1827):

> There were few men in this country who did not agree that the war declared by America was unprovoked on our part, [but] ... that person must have singular views of the policy of Great Britain, who should think that it ought to be continued by us for the purpose of territorial aggrandizement, or from vindictive feelings. Our sole object was to resist aggression, and to support our maritime rights. We had gloriously defended Canada, had surrendered no rights, and had made a peace in the spirit of peace, which would open again a wide field for the commerce and manufactures of this country....[40]

For his part, President Madison claimed victory. With the defeat of Napoleon, such Maritime grievances as impressment, blockade, definition of contraband, and the rights of neutrals had become academic, at least for the foreseeable future. As he presented copies of the Treaty of Ghent to the United States Senate, the President said: "I congratulate you and our constituents upon an event which is highly honorable to the nation and terminates, with peculiar felicity, a campaign signalized by the most brilliant successes." Madison welcomed peace "at a period when the causes for the war have ceased to operate; when the Government has demonstrated the efficiency of its powers of defence; and when the nation can review its conduct without regret and without reproach." He did not mention Mackinac Island nor any other military setbacks.[41]

Chapter VI

Aftermath of the War of 1812

The Treaty of Ghent obliged each of the belligerents, Great Britain and the United States, to return to the pre-war boundaries — whatever they were. News took months to travel from Ghent, in Belgium, in large part due to the difficulties weather conditions posed to shipping during winter months. Official notification passed from Ghent, to London, to York (Toronto) to the British commander on Mackinac Island, Lieutenant-Colonel Robert McDouall (who succeeded Bullock on 18 May 1814). The courier handed the papers to McDouall 11 May 1815. In accord with the Treaty of Ghent, British forces left Mackinac Island 18 July 1815, and the US Army re-established its presence there.

There was no question but that the British would have to leave, but where would they go? One consideration had to be Amerindian opinion. First, McDouall realized that some of the Indians who had helped to capture Mackinac Island might be angry about its return to American hands. He wanted them fed and presented with a greater number of gifts than would usually have been the case before the British withdrawal.[1] Also, if there was to be a British presence — let alone a profitable fur trade — on the Upper Great Lakes, Great Britain had to maintain credibility with the people who lived there. A return to Fort St. Joseph was a possibility, especially as the North West Company and Astor had buildings there that had survived the war.[2] As late as mid-May 1815, McDouall expected to return to St. Joseph Island. He wrote:

> The repairs of the buildings at St. Josephs are rapidly going on, & if necessary will soon be fit to receive the Garrison and Stores. I have for that purpose made use of the dwelling house & store-houses of the Southwest Company;... occupy them we must if this Island [Mackinac] is speedily given up.[3]

On 17 May, McDouall made a similar statement and indicated that he had already sent provisions from Mackinac to St. Joseph Island.[4] As late as February 1816, the British garrison's magazine remained at Fort St. Joseph.[5]

However, given the importance of Fort Mackinac as the guardian of the approaches to three Great Lakes, *it* was obviously the place to watch. Drummond Island was geographically closer to Mackinac Island than was Fort St. Joseph. Moreover, there was no guarantee that St. Joseph Island would remain in British hands. McDouall certainly did not think so.[6] If ownership of the islands remained to be resolved — as it did — it seemed sensible to build the fort on the most useful island and worry about the future as it unfolded. Drummond Island too remained a question mark, but meanwhile it could serve British interests well. By 24 June, McDouall and his officers had determined that Drummond Island was preferable to Fort St. Joseph, Sault Ste. Marie, or any other site in the area. They named the island after Sir

Gordon Drummond, then the administrator (acting lieutenant-governor) of Upper Canada.

Another factor in the move to Drummond Island was the dreary state of Fort St. Joseph. David Wingfield, a naval officer who viewed the location in May 1815, wrote:

> The Americans had entirely destroyed the fort, if it was ever worthy of such a name, the barracks and several of the houses, and but two or three of those which were left were tenantable, as the Lake had risen three feet above its usual height, and the lower part was covered with water; at this time there were no inhabitants.[7]

McDouall certainly had no intention of remaining on St. Joseph Island, and by early August he had moved his men to Drummond Island. Except for the South West Company's three buildings, spared by the American raiders, all that remained on St. Joseph Island were a collection of ruins, the keen stench of fired structures, and a few men, living in stabilized ruins, to guard the stores and the Indian Department's establishment. The principal responsibility of these last was to smooth the edge of Indian resentment by a generous distribution of presents and careful attention to the requisite ceremonies. That season, John Askin dressed some 1,500 Indians.[8]

McDouall's choice of Drummond Island over Fort St. Joseph (in spite of his apprehension that the boundary commissioners might declare Drummond to be US territory) further exposed the unsuitability of the latter. The site on Drummond commanded the Detour entrance to the St. Mary's River, and offered the shelter of a good harbour, which Fort St. Joseph patently lacked. Also driving his determination was the need to select a site as close to Mackinac as possible, in order to sustain some influence over the Indians attracted to the Strait, and to support the interest of the South Western fur traders, including William McGillivray, later chief director of the North West Company. Indeed, McGillivray had informed Prevost that the engineering officers who had surveyed the St. Mary's River and its approaches in search of the most suitable site for a fort could not agree whether Drummond was preferable to a site near the falls. At any rate, St. Joseph was unsuitable. McGillivray recognized the island's agricultural potential but regarded it as inappropriate for a military post.[9]

British authorities purchased the South West Company's buildings, including two good storehouses, on a point to the east of Fort St. Joseph, for half price. They then physically relocated at least one of these buildings to Drummond Island. By late September 1815, the transfer process was all but complete.[10] Only a few soldiers remained on St. Joseph Island to guard the powder in the magazine and watch over the small herd of cattle pastured there.[11] After an inspection tour of 1816, Lieutenant-Colonel E.W. Durnford of the British Army recommended the transfer of the balance of the powder, for the magazine at Fort St. Joseph was deteriorating, and the storage site at such a distance from Drummond Island obliged the British Army to keep some of its soldiers there, a most inefficient use of limited personnel. Somewhat later, Lieutenant J.E. Portlock found all the remaining buildings either degraded, stripped of salvageable parts, or unstable to the point of requiring props.[12]

An inventory of the buildings drafted in 1826 confirms the irrelevance into which Fort St. Joseph had fallen:

A Stone building with a shingled roof, the arched ceiling [of which] is much cracked.

A brick building with a good oven — It was formerly covered with sheet Iron but that having been removed it has now a barked Roof — It is occupied as a Barrack by the Guard left at St Josephs to protect the Magazine. —

This belonged originally to the N. West Company and was purchased by the Government, it is of a similar nature to that brought over and now occupied by the commissariat — The roof has suffered exceedingly: and Props have been placed against the walls to secure them from falling — The floors are good — This store is used only as a Cattle Stable & Hay loft. —

Bought also from the N. West Company & brought from St Josephs in 1820 the Finished house lies on the ground [at Drummond Island] and (in my opinion) would have been better left standing at St Josephs — some of it now rotten. —

It may be generally observed that the Buildings are rapidly progressing to decay and that (even were the Post retained) it would be necessary in some few years to build others of a more permanent nature.[13]

The civilian population of St. Joseph Island followed the military to Drummond Island. Whatever charms St. Joseph might have had, they could not compete with the alternatives.[14]

Meanwhile, military life continued on Drummond Island. Whether the British selected the best site on Drummond Island is not altogether clear. According to historian Samuel Fletcher Cook, they located their fort on the eastern side of Drummond Island, "in a locality which seems to have been chosen more on account of its beauty than for its value for military strategy."[15] The site is now private property not readily accessible to tourists, but Cook says that the British soldiers had large buildings with huge fireplaces. The British built these structures to last. There were others of a more temporary nature, although pleasant while they endured.[16]

By the time the British left in 1828, there were twenty buildings.[17] Cook says:

When Col. T.L. McKenney, the traveler and writer on indian [sic] affairs, visited the place in 1827,... he found the post surgeon, who had recently arrived from London with a young bride,... seemingly contented with his home and its appointments.[18]

According to Cook, the garrison's buildings were "unusually large for log houses, and were almost more scattered than was usual in those days for military posts."[19] There were parade grounds beside the water, and barracks and a commissary near a rocky hill on the western border. As usual, the officers had separate quarters, and as had been the case as Fort St. Joseph, the garrison at Drummond Island had its own cemetery.[20]

From Cook's account, it is evident that this was no temporary post, built to strengthen British claims in any boundary dispute. Contemporary correspondence, however, indicates a tug-of-war between those who had to live on Drummond Island and those who remained in Quebec. The former wanted functional buildings; the latter stressed economy. They would spend the minimum until the boundary commission had determined who owned which islands.[21]

An undated report written in 1820 or shortly thereafter indicated that those who favoured economy prevailed. The report describes Drummond Island's buildings:

> Barrack: A log Building with Shingled roof ceiling of Boards, Walls pointed both on the out and inside. The rain and snow penetrate the Walls and in some places the roof; a covering of Bark would be necessary to secure the former. The Floor also requires some repair.

> Barrack: A building similar to the preceding one with the exception of its roof which is covered with Bark not with shingles — & requires exactly the same repairs — Half only of this building is occupied as a Barrack the remainder is used as a guard room —

Artillery Barracks: A frame & log Building pointed on the out & inside — Roof covered with Bark the Rain and Snow pass through the Walls and some small places in the roof- -Repair of a nature similar to that required by the other Barracks will be necessary. The floor is good. —

Hospital: A log Building with mortar Roof of Bark — the roof needs repair and the Walls a covering of Bark. Some of the Windows, also, should be attended too. —

Barrack Masters Store: This adjoins the Hospital and originally formed part of it. It was built with Similar materials and needs still more extensive repairs. —

Commissariat Provision Store: A post, and log Building with a floor of lattened logs — this was an old store (of the N. West Company) purchased by Government It had originally an upper floor which is now but partly laid having been put up without judgment, it has become on one side very much inclined and is now supported by ropes and Chains, Some of the Posts have been split but with all these defects it will probably last as long as is now necessary — The roof requires repair. —

Ordnance Store: A post and Log Building just fitted up as an Engineer Store but transferred by order of Major Winnett Comm to the ordnance Roof Shingled — the Walls do not keep out the Rain and therefore Should be barked — it is generally in a good state. —

Commissariat Store for Stores: A post and log Building. The Walls and roof are covered with bark the latter requires some little repair — There is a loft floor and altho props have been found necessary to ensure Security it is still a Serviceable Building. —

Barrack and Kitchen: A post and log Building with a roof of Bark The Chimnies smoke exceedingly and the Walls require Repair. —

Commissariat Store for provisions: A post and log Building with a log floor and a barked roof Props have been found necessary but the Building (although but wretched is still useful. Some repairs are necessary —

Commissariat Store: Formerly this was an officers Quarter but having been examined and condemned it is now used as a store for lime, Charcoal, and some other articles —

Mess House: A post and log building lathed and plastered on the inside The Roof is shingled, It was originally the Engineer Quarter and consists of three rooms adjoining is a Kitchen — The Roof of the house leaks in some places but that of the kitchen everywhere. —

Commanding Officers Quarters: A frame house weather boarded and connected by a passage with a post & log Building used as a kitchen & both have shingled Roofs The principal House consists of three rooms on the ground & two on the attic Floor, The other of a kitchen and two small rooms both are in good order. —

Commissariat Stable: The timbers of the floor were laid down in 1816 and those of the Walls prepared while any further progress was stopped by order of His Excellency Sir John C. Sherbrooke G.C.B. —

Block House: In 1820 a fire destroyed the timber of the Walls & much other timber — What remains is yet sound and may at any time be advantageously removed. — [22]

The same report tabled what was left at Fort St. Joseph, quickly becoming derelict. Although not totally abandoned by the military, it would, presumably, have been in better shape had all the soldiers returned there and not diverted their energy to Drummond Island.

Magazine: A Stone building with a shingled roof the arched ceiling is much cracked.

Bake House: A brick building with a good oven — It was formerly covered with sheet Iron but that having been removed it has now a barked Roof — It is occupied as a Barrack by the Guard left at St. Josephs to protect the Magazine. —

Store House: This belonged originally to the N. West Company and was purchased by Government, it is of a similar nature to that brought over and now occupied by the commissariat — The Roof has suffered exceedingly: and Props have been placed against the walls to secure them from falling — The floors are good — This store is only used as a Cattle Stable & Hay loft. —

House: Bought also from the N. West Company & bought [brought?] from St. Josephs in 1820 The Finished house lies on the ground and (in my opinion) would have much better been left standing at St. Josephs — some of it is now rotten —

> Observation: It may be generally observed that the Buildings are rapidly progressing to decay and that (even were the Post retained) it would be necessary in some few years to build others of a more permanent nature — [23]

By the summer of 1818, some civilians sought to settle as farmers or merchants on St. Joseph Island. Some even claimed to have bought land. Although he recognized that St. Joseph Island had huge tracts of "excellent land" suitable for farming and cattle raising, Major Thomas Howard of the 70th Regiment, then on Drummond Island, attached no credibility to the land claims and discouraged immediate settlement. "No person resides on the Island except a Corporals [sic] guard for the protection of the Magazine," he said.[24] One can but speculate as to the future development of Northeastern Ontario had the settlers gained permission to settle, especially if the military base had remained at Fort St. Joseph. St. Joseph Island, after all, remained British territory. Drummond Island did not. A fort at St. Joseph Island would likely have stimulated development of an adjacent civilian population, and it need not have moved out of the region after 1828.

While Article II of the 1783 Treaty of Paris specifically designated the north shore of the Great Lakes and connecting waterways to Great Britain and the south shore to the United States, it did not deal with the islands. The exact wording was that the boundary should pass

> through the middle of said lake [Lake Huron] to the Water Communication [the St. Mary's River] between that Lake and Lake Superior.

British authorities hoped that they might exploit the ambiguity so that Drummond Island could be British.

Article VI of the Treaty of Ghent dealt with this omission.

Article VI noted that "doubts have arisen [as to] what was the middle of the said River, Lakes, and water communications, and whether certain Islands lying in the same were within the Dominions of His Britannic Majesty or of the United States." In order to resolve this matter, the two parties agreed to appoint two commissioners to determine ownership. Their decisions had to be compatible with the spirit of the 1783 settlement, and their decisions would be binding.

It was not until 1822 that the commission actually undertook its work, and when it did, one of its first decisions was that no island would be divided. Each island would be entirely British or entirely American. A subsequent decision concluded that Bois Blanc Island (near Detroit) should be British while the United States would possess Drummond Island.[25]

The strategy required to safeguard ongoing British interests in the North American interior now came under review by a commission led by Major-General Sir James Carmichael Smyth. The Smyth Commission rejected the Canadian Sault Ste. Marie because, in order to reach it, ships would have had to pass directly beneath the guns of the US Fort Brady on the opposite shore. (The US Army began to build Fort Brady on the waterfront of the American Sault Ste. Marie in 1822.) Smyth wanted a harbour that would not be icebound several months each year. He thought the geography of Fort St. Joseph ideal, but the cost of its reconstruction would have been formidable.[26]

British authorities selected Penetanguishene, where the Royal Navy already had an establishment. (The naval base lasted until 1834, the army base until 1856.) The British garrison then vacated Drummond in such haste and so late in the season that many soldiers suffered a significant loss of property.[27] The formal surrender of Drummond Island to Lieutenant T. Pierce Simonton of the US Army base at Fort Brady took place 14 November 1828. British willingness to leave Drummond Island, where they had invested so heavily, indicates a strong desire for peace. The trip from Drummond Island to Penetanguishene proved quite miserable for the seven officers, forty men of the ranks, fifteen women, twenty-six children, and three servants. The unfortunate ninety-one set sail 16 November in the midst of a snowstorm and travelled five days aboard two vessels through rough water.[28]

Graeme Mount and Andre Laferriere standing outside the reconstructed buildings at Penetanguishene, successor to Fort St. Joseph and Fort Drummond.
Photo by Michael J. Mulloy, 1998

Hence, the army joined the navy in Penetanguishene. In 1793, the year before the signing of Jay's Treaty, Lieutenant-Governor Simcoe had suggested construction of a naval base there. His idea was that supplies could travel overland from York to Penetanguishene, out of range of American guns and ships. Safely at Penetanguishene, the goods could then travel to British posts around the Upper Great Lakes. In 1797, one year after Simcoe's term as

Lieutenant-Governor had ended, British authorities purchased the Penetanguishene Peninsula from the Chippewa nation, but they did not actually locate the naval establishment there at that time. After all, there was a lessening of tensions after the conclusion of Jay's Treaty, and Great Britain was facing the challenges of revolutionary France.

However, during the War of 1812 the advantages of a supply depot and naval dockyard on Georgian Bay became patently obvious. Such a facility was indispensable to the supplying of the British soldiers who occupied Mackinac Island. After the war, it was equally vital to the garrison on Drummond Island. An army presence at Penetanguishene would have definite advantages as well. Again, supplies could travel overland from Toronto, up Yonge Street — now Highway 11 — to Lake Simcoe, across Lake Simcoe, and west along what is now Highway 12 to the Midland-

A replica of the HMS *Tecumseth*, a schooner in use at the Penetanguishene army and navy base. Ships like this transported passengers and freight on the Great Lakes during the first half of the nineteenth century.
Photo by Michael J. Mulloy, 1998

Penetanguishene region. Moreover, an army base at Penetanguishene might attract settlers to the region. Those settlers could form a militia that would assist the army in defending Upper Canada from possible American attack.

Original stone building used by officers at Fort Penetanguishene. *Photo by Michael J. Mulloy, 1998*

Some of the reconstructed buildings at Fort Penetanguishene. *Photo by Michael J. Mulloy, 1998*

Student archaeologists from the University of Waterloo excavate Fort Penetanguishene.
Photo by Michael J. Mulloy, 1998

Did it matter militarily that the army built its base at Penetanguishene rather than at Fort St. Joseph? In 1817, acting Secretary of State Richard Rush and the British Minister in Washington, Lord Bagot, concluded the Rush-Bagot Agreement affecting naval disarmament on the Great Lakes and Lake Champlain. Unless either side gave six months notice of abrogation, henceforth each side would be restricted to one warship on Lake Champlain, one on Lake Ontario, and two on the remaining Great Lakes combined. The apparent success of the Rush-Bagot Agreement led to the closure of the naval establishment at Penetanguishene in 1834, three years before the Upper Canadian rebellion of 1837 led to the first violations.

In 1845–1846 there was a war scare as the belligerent US President James Knox Polk (1845–1849) claimed "all Oregon" and threatened to enforce his claim by military action; "all Oregon" included what are now the states of Oregon and Washington, as well as the province of British Columbia. Even had there not been a peaceful resolution to that problem, it is doubtful whether a British military presence at Fort St. Joseph (rather than at Penetanguishene) would have benefited the British cause. Surely, if neither party abrogated the Rush-Bagot Agreement (most unlikely!), belligerents would have concentrated their limited resources on the most heavily populated areas. If either side did abrogate the arrangement, the United States could probably have won any naval armaments race. It had more people on the shores of the Great Lakes than did the British, and the British Navy could not sail past the St. Lawrence rapids between Montreal and Kingston. By 1837 Michigan had sufficient population to achieve statehood, 212,267 by the time of the census of 1840. There would have been numerous people willing to defend their state against any offensive action launched by a few score people from Fort St. Joseph. At the same time, the few hundred people in the Canadian Sault Ste. Marie would hardly have been a match for the hundreds of thousands on the other side of the border.

Finally, even the British Army base at Penetanguishene closed before the outbreak of the US Civil War in 1861, the last occasion when an Anglo-American War appeared a serious threat. The 1871 Treaty of Washington guaranteed that there would be no war, and the undefended boundary dates from that time. Wise statesmanship and some good luck rather than a British garrison at any particular location proved decisive between 1861 and 1871.

Chapter VII

Breathing Life Into an Ancient Corpse —
Glyn Smith and the Campaign to Revive Fort St. Joseph

While several families remained in residence on the southern part of St. Joseph Island, it was not until 1834 that Major William Rains of the British Army and promoters Charles Thompson and Archibald Hamilton Scott advanced a scheme to colonize the island. Despite their initial efforts, which involved construction of a sawmill and store in the southeast, immigrants to Upper Canada preferred more southerly latitudes. Rains moved his family to the point that now bears his name and constructed buildings on the site of the South West Company's establishment. There he remained until 1849, an object of great curiosity for educated travellers following the old water route to the northwest.[1]

Yet, some people did go to St. Joseph Island, as transients and as settlers. They picked berries and manufactured maple syrup, some to be preserved for subsistence, some to be sold commercially. They fished. As the mineral resources of Lake Superior developed in the 1840s and the Sault Ste. Marie

Canal began operations in 1855, steamship traffic on the St. Mary's increased. The island's forests were made-to-order for burning under the steamers' boilers, and cutting cordwood and hauling it to docks on the west side of the island for use on steamships was the principal economic activity until the 1870s, when agriculture became more important. The fort itself remained undisturbed, since it was a boulder-ridden knoll on the isolated southwestern tip of the island, surrounded by swamp.

In 1922, a request for permission to cut timber raised interest in the fort. Although it later turned out that the site of Fort St. Joseph was not the loggers' target, this proposal to alter the status quo stimulated agitation for a freeze on any kind of development until the federal government's Historical Sites and Monuments Board could evaluate the site. The mild shock did prompt a series of low-level responses involving investigations, some stabilization, and the appointment of a custodian. In 1923, the *Sault Star* revealed that the Sault Ste. Marie Historical Society planned an expedition to the grounds. The excursion took place the following year. From this ensued several suggestions for remedial work. The federal government responded by financing repairs on masonry structures in 1926 and transferring the surrounding land to the National Parks Branch. In 1928, it erected a commemorative tablet and appointed a caretaker. There were additional repairs to the stonework in the 1930s.

Interest and activity increased after World War II, in part because of the leadership of Glyn Smith, an energetic native of St. Joseph Island and an enthusiastic local historian. The campaign to raise the fort's profile, even to exploit any economic opportunities that it might offer, led to a letter-writing campaign to the local Member of Parliament, George Nixon (Liberal — Algoma West). Nixon, in turn, asked questions in the House of Commons. There were articles in the *Sault Star*. As a result of this campaign, federal authorities built a road to the fort and a parking lot, picnic tables, and fireplaces at the fort. In 1948 there was a celebration of the sesquicentennial of the British Army's purchase of St. Joseph Island in 1798. In 1954, the Government of Canada erected a cairn and plaque to mark the fort's graveyard. Finally, in an act that signified that henceforth the fort was to be taken seriously as a historic site, the National and Historic Parks Branch financed an archaeological expedition, undertaken by the Department of Anthropology at the University of Toronto in 1963 and 1964. In these years before Canada's centennial, Canadians were showing a renewed interest in their history, and Fort St. Joseph — like Louisbourg on Cape Breton Island — benefitted.

The University of Toronto team excavated buildings, traced lines of palisades, and surveyed the area of the fort. Almost a decade later, in 1973, the Government of Canada

Student archaeologists from the University of Toronto begin the excavation of Fort St. Joseph in the summer of 1963.
Photo by Parks Canada photographer D.K. Hakas

transferred the adjacent Ordnance and Naval Reserves, preserved until then as a bird sanctuary, to the National and Historic Parks branch.[2]

One of the minor mysteries associated with the rehabilitation of Fort St. Joseph has to be Glyn Smith's motives. Contrasted with such establishments as Louisbourg and Mackinac — which remained a US Army base for most of the nineteenth century — the history of Fort St. Joseph was brief. It was a hinterland establishment, reluctantly and somewhat shabbily constructed only after the terms of Jay's Treaty terminated British occupation of Fort Mackinac. Even when it was an active military base, Fort St. Joseph never replaced Mackinac as the centre of the fur trade. Given the modest size of both the fort and the garrison, Fort St. Joseph's viability depended upon the good will of the western tribes. Fortunately, they tended to be well disposed toward the British who, at worst, they regarded as the least evil of all realistic options. Also, Spartan as conditions were, Fort St. Joseph did succeed in its one moment of crisis. (The much more opulent Louisbourg failed.)

The decision to re-establish the outpost of British influence on the Upper Great Lakes to Drummond Island, then to Penetanguishene, was a matter of considerable chagrin to Smith. Military spending stimulated the economy of Simcoe County, while that of St. Joseph Island languished. Glyn Smith was an enthusiastic historian. For such people, the paper chase is a thrilling experience that creates a story from documents. In practice, however, Smith realized that there had to be a heritage industry if tourist spending was to refertilize an exhausted island economy. He understood that the agriculture- and resource-based economy of St. Joseph Island could not compete with that of Sault Ste. Marie or southern Ontario. Accordingly, residents of the island had to cultivate a tourist industry and attract money from travellers and campers.

The essentials of Glyn Smith's campaign to raise the profile of Fort St. Joseph emerged in a letter from S.A.

Wallace, a Windsor barrister, late in the summer of 1949. Smith's strategy required the formation of an island historical society to focus and channel local interest and energy, and to associate the fort's advocates with the Ontario Historical Society, whose very charter required it to preserve and promote the province's past. Membership in this organization would offer islanders opportunities to secure influential allies in their campaign to promote their cause and attract tourists.

Wallace, who knew St. Joseph Island well, sought the advice of George McDonald, president of the Essex County Historical Society. McDonald advised Smith to form a distinct society; membership in already existing organizations at Sault Ste. Marie or Windsor would simply put the island's project into competition with hometown causes. Wallace was enthusiastic about McDonald's potential for assistance in the cause. "That man," he exclaimed, "knows more about the History of St. Joe's Island than you and I together.... That man is a wissard [sic] on Ontario Historical sites, it is his hobby, he could fill a musieum [sic] with his collections." Wallace himself intended to research and write an article on the fort for the *Windsor Star*, complete with photographs he and Smith had taken.[3]

Two months later, Wallace wrote an apology for failing to return Smith's photographs and complete his article for the *Windsor Star*. His own photographs had turned out well and he had done considerable research, but his wife's illness had taken his time, and his lodge responsibilities had stymied him for the moment. Yet, he retained a strong interest in their shared objective, which was "to get recognition from the Government to make the old Fort Grounds a tourist attraction."

He had discovered, however, that piquing the government's interest and enlisting it as a reliable ally and funding agency would require effort. His conversation with the provincial Planning and Development Department at the Canadian National Exhibition in Toronto had revealed total ignorance of the fort: nobody had a clue that it existed. To rectify this problem, Wallace intended to submit copies of his articles to those government officials responsible for tourist development in Ontario, and to write England for a list of the soldiers buried in the fort's graveyard. He gratefully acknowledged Smith's assistance in guiding him around the site and providing him with information and photographs. Their mutual desire, he said, was "to get that place into the public mind for what it means to Canada, and the Soldierrs [*sic*] who served there, and saved the day for us in the war of 1812."[4]

Another part of Smith's strategy required the support of the regional military establishment, a sound decision given the fort's association with the defence of Canada, as well as the strength and influence of the Royal Canadian Legion and local militias so soon after World War II. Smith found a very helpful ally in Louis Derrer, the influential commanding officer of the 49th Heavy Anti-Aircraft Regiment in Sault Ste. Marie. On 2 September 1948, Lieutenant-Colonel Derrer thanked Smith for his blueprint of the fort. From that he found information that was useful for the upcoming sesquicentennial celebrations. After the actual celebrations, which took place 19 September, Derrer sent Smith a letter containing two photographs taken at the sesquicentennial and offered to do what he could to promote the fort and what it represented. Respect for the location, he said, required an extensive buffer around the site itself, but it was possible that the government might sell adjacent land "for tourist purposes." Derrer informed Smith that he had written to the local member of Parliament, George Nixon, opposing any such move, and he hoped that Nixon had approached the Department of Mines and Developments to block such a development. Derrer said that several reeves from communities on St. Joseph Island agreed with him and had written similar letters.[5]

An act of genius was what ultimately safeguarded the ruins and their environs. Smith and his supporters petitioned the federal government to declare the site a bird sanctuary (and thereby preserve its integrity). Nixon acknowledged Smith's letter 13 September 1950 and the same day forwarded it to Robert Winters, Minister of Resources and Development in the cabinet of Prime Minister Louis St. Laurent.[6] On 8 March 1951, an Order-in-Council proclaimed that the entire Ordnance Reserve Number One (a Military Reserve) and the entire Naval Reserve lettered A in concession A, Jocelyn Township, along with the offshore waters, reefs, and islands, should become the St. Joseph Island Bird Sanctuary.[7] Nixon attached this order to a letter and commented that the designation process had not been an easy one. On the contrary, he said, the happy outcome was the product of "much effort and lengthy consultation."[8]

In his letter of appreciation for Nixon's assistance, Smith perhaps expressed his belief that the preservation of a people's history was really the responsibility of a few enthusiasts. Most people, he thought, really were indifferent. At best, their interest in historical projects and the historical process was sporadic and ephemeral. He and the true believers had to assume that Canadians would eventually come to value their history; preserving the integrity of the fort's site was thus a blow in the interests of posterity. He admitted that some of the island's hunters had not surrendered their haunts with good grace, but he noted that they could still pursue their sport over much of the island.

Determined promoter that he was, Smith ignored Nixon's message about difficulties and asked Nixon whether he might drop into the Parks Board office and ask what the programme would be for the summer of 1951. He agreed with Nixon that the islanders were not militant supporters of the cause, although Smith expressed the belief that they were supporters, in their own quiet ways. Surely, he reasoned, once they had experienced the miraculous impact of American dollars, they would come on side. He informed

Nixon that he had done some research that suggested their efforts had achieved a degree of success. At his request, islander Louis Adcock had done a count on two Sundays. The first week ninety-seven vehicles appeared at the site, the following week 110. Many had foreign plates, "and that means money, not to us, but to someone, and eventually this condition will be realized and people on the Island will know that ... they have an increasing and everlasting small tourist mine on their Island."[9]

If the fort was to become an incubator for the tourist industry and a stimulus for Canadians to take an interest in their history, it could not remain an isolated, desolate bird sanctuary. There must be plans for "rehabilitation," and such plans must necessarily include improved access to the site. On 8 January 1949, Smith had written Nixon about appropriations to initiate "rehabilitation." Would it help if the local Legion branch requested the Dominion Command of the Legion to press the Department? Grateful as he was for Nixon's efforts, the task required more than money.

Smith noted expenditures upon Fort Frontenac at Kingston. The Ontario Department of Highways spent $250,000 to enhance the transportation infrastructure there, and some 90,000 visitors had gone to the fort over the summer of 1948. According to Immigration statistics, he continued, 300,000 Americans crossed the border at Sault Ste. Marie into Canada each year. They must have had some expectations. Was the Sault Chamber of Commerce not missing the boat in its failure to promote attractions such as Fort St. Joseph,

> instead of leaving it to a few of us to work our heads off? Historically this Algoma area can offer tourist attractions that few places in Canada can better, yet it is not done. We should get out proper folders and pamphlets to be given visitors, yet in

the case of Fort St. Joseph the work is not far
enough advanced to do the place justice.

Rest assured, Smith concluded, he appreciated Nixon's
efforts, but surely as "a willing horse" he would not object
to "a little more load."[10]

In the House of Commons, Nixon had a reputation as
"Silent George." However, in the back rooms and in the
offices of cabinet ministers, he earned the respect of
many constituents. On 1 February 1949, Nixon wrote to
James Mackinnon, Minister of Mines and Resources,
thanking him and his department for building the road to
the fort the previous summer and urging him to keep up
the good work:

> If this site was improved, such as beautifying and
> building a road around the actual site itself, the
> attraction to American tourists would be so great
> that from a U.S. dollar standpoint alone it is indeed
> worthy of consideration.[11]

On 5 August 1950 Smith informed Nixon that he had
been talking with John T. Stubbs, a Sault Ste. Marie high
school teacher who was also an officer in the 49th. Smith had
asked Stubbs to enquire as to which department held title to
the Military and Naval Reserves. He wanted to know because
the Department of Mines and Resources was building a
perimeter road around the fort. (If, he inserted, that was due
to Nixon's efforts, he would see that the Member of
Parliament received credit in the local newspaper.) Smith
noted that there was a gap of five miles (eight kilometres)
between the provincial road around the perimeter of the island
and the federal road at the fort. The municipality was too
impoverished to build the connector, although such a road
would normally be its responsibility. If there were to be a
campaign to convince the province to build the road, "we
should know the facts and angles."

On 25 June 1950, Communist North Korean forces invaded South Korea, and the war began catastrophically. As North Korean forces launched their southward offensive and pushed US and South Korean forces into the tiny corner that military historians now label "the Pusan Perimeter," Smith invoked the Cold War as a reason for developing Fort St. Joseph.

> I know this business does not get or stir local and district interest the way it should but someone has to plant the acorn. People ... have to be taught to take an interest in the history of their country, and do you know of any other way to do it?... The only stand against Communism to date has been by Tito [Communist leader of Yugoslavia who had defied Stalin], and how did he do it except by appealing to the pride and nationalism of the Jugo Slavs. To get to the point, you just have to teach it.[12]

That same summer, Bob Farquharson, the Managing Editor of *The Globe and Mail*, had vacationed on St. Joseph Island. Smith managed to convince him of the island's relevance, and Farquharson wrote to C.W. Jackson, Assistant Deputy Minister of the Department of Resources and Development. Jackson replied that the road built the previous year was but the first step in a series of road construction projects around the site.[13]

Jackson meant what he said. On 26 April 1951, Nixon forwarded a copy of a letter he had received from Robert Winters about development at the fort. It contained the agenda of improvements for 1951. In order to preserve the dermatological integrity of visiting tourists, the caretaker had to eradicate the poison ivy. Workers would build four toilets and three picnic tables, repair the chimney, and erect signs.[14]

On 22 January 1953 Smith wrote to Nixon again. Nixon was a Liberal who supported the Liberal government of Louis St. Laurent, but Smith praised the provincial Progressive

Conservative government led by Leslie Frost. They had, Smith said, discharged their responsibility nobly, and through the works programme of the Ontario Department of Highways had significantly improved communication between St. Joseph Island and the mainland. Smith anticipated a larger infusion of visitors. Accordingly, he asked, had the time not come to ask Mines and Resources to augment the tiny expenditures made by the Parks Board?

> As you know the present Fort road only encloses half the Fort peninsula, and completing the remaining half would be a great improvement. The stone buildings should also have a start made on them to prevent further deterioration.

Smith asked Nixon to seek four thousand dollars, half for the road and half for building repairs.[15]

Smith gave speeches on the importance of Fort St. Joseph to Canadian history. In his campaign to raise both the islanders' consciousness and their ire, he excoriated the British government for surrendering what he considered Canadian territory (the lands between the Ohio and Mississippi rivers) in the negotiations of 1783, and Canadian educational authorities who denied recognition to those who deserved the nation's gratitude. He thought that the latter ignored or minimized the achievements of Captain Roberts and his men:

> The early move of Captain Roberts and subsequent capture of Mackinaw [sic] from the St Joseph outpost was one of the decisive moves in holding the Canadian positions in the War of 1812. It can be said that this war was the birth pangs of the Canadian nation. Even a cursory study of history will prove that statement.... We ... who live in this area have a legitimate grievance against our schools and educational authorities in their treatment of

> Canadian History.... St. Joseph Island has never received a fair deal in our schools or history books and it [is] up to the people like ourselves to try and correct this error.

He was angry that British authorities had negotiated the Treaty of Ghent, which returned Mackinac Island to the United States. As far he was concerned, the British compounded their error when they failed to restore Fort St. Joseph. The islanders could do something about this, he believed.[16]

One may argue that Smith exaggerated the importance of the Roberts expedition and minimized the difficulties of ending the War of 1812 and restoring Fort St. Joseph, but *he* believed what he said and took action. In 1954, he received a newspaper article about the restoration of the naval and military bases at Penetanguishene and what it meant to the local economy. Its author, Norman Riddiough of the *London Free Press*, suggested that what Penetanguishene had done, other small Ontario communities might profitably do as well, and to illustrate his point he cited Midland, site of Ste. Marie among the Hurons.[17] That very autumn, Smith took his campaign into the offices of Provincial Archivist George W. Sprague. Surely, he counselled Sprague, the capture of Mackinac Island was *the* key event in the entire War of 1812. With the exception of Fred Landon, Southern Ontario historians had overlooked its significance. The capture of Mackinac confirmed Indian support for the British cause. Prior to that, Tecumseh had only a handful of followers. When news of Mackinac's capture reached Brock at York, it altered the morale of members of the militia who had been agitating to return to their farms. Now they were willing to serve anywhere in the province. Brock could take Detroit only because the Indians had rallied to Tecumseh. Detroit provided the arms and ordnance that enabled a previously underequipped force to face the Americans along the Niagara frontier.[18]

Smith confronted Landon. The successful raid on Mackinac, he argued, had undermined US strategy, for it put into play a train of events that ultimately annihilated the third prong of a three-prong attack on Canada. Why, he asked Landon, did historians emphasize the Niagara Frontier and ignore what was happening in the northwest? The answer, he insinuated, was that more historians lived closer to the Niagara Peninsula than to St. Joseph Island.[19] Landon replied that he had given the Mackinac events considerable space in his book, *Lake Huron*, but that he could not have said everything that it was possible to say.[20]

Glyn Smith had a point, but the emphasis on the Niagara Frontier is not difficult to understand. American attacks across the Niagara River directly threatened the Upper Canadian heartland. For his part, Smith ignored an event at least as significant as the victory at Mackinac — the naval Battle of Lake Erie at Put-in-Bay that opened the way for the American expedition that torched Fort St. Joseph. While Smith sought credit for Roberts, he gave the impression that he also sought to diminish events on the Niagara Frontier. That, of course, is a common error among the fervently committed.

Smith also complained that Americans, to their credit, gloried in their history while Canadians ignored their own past. Fort St. Joseph, he hoped, might become a symbol of Canadian nationalism. The population discrepancy, 10:1 in favour of the United States, had given the United States more to remember and more resources with which to remember the past, but he felt very strongly that Canadians could have done more than they had done.[21]

When dealing with Nixon, a Liberal, Smith had praised the behaviour of Ontario's Progressive Conservative government. However, he had serious problems with Queen's Park and chose to combat what he considered sloth and ignorance in the Ontario Department of Travel and Publicity. He noted a serious error in one of its guides that said that two American vessels, the *Tigress* and the

Scorpion, had been captured at Nottawasaga Creek 3 and 6 September 1814. Such was not the case, he said.

> They were captured at St. Joseph Island and in the vicinity of Fort St. Joseph.... When a person finds certain facts in error, then the whole pamphlet becomes suspect....[22]

In reply, the Deputy Minister (Crowe) thanked Smith and announced a new pamphlet of thirty-six pages on Ontario's history.

Smith was indignant. How, he observed, could one squeeze Ontario's history into a mere thirty-six pages? He offered his services as a consultant with regard to St. Joseph Island, the fort, and the military actions of 1812 and 1814 around Fort Mackinac. At the same time, he blasted two officials from the Deputy Minister's department who had rejected his offer to serve as their guide when they visited St. Joseph Island on the grounds that they wished to view the area as if they were common tourists. "If your department is responsible for the advancement [of] historical interest from the visitor's point of view, then your files must be a repository of every last scrap of information that can be obtained," he wrote.[23]

Smith also regarded the Department of Education with contempt. History, which could have been "an enthralling story from even the kindergarten," was taught in a most boring way, as a mass of forgettable dry statistics. Patriotism can work miracles, he argued. Stalin had abandoned his emphasis on ideology, resorted to patriotism, and motivated his people to fight against Hitler. Tito had capitalized upon Yugoslav patriotism. The collective Canadian will would be stronger if Canadians appreciated their history, and Fort St. Joseph could be a means of building that appreciation.[24]

Smith's enthusiasm for historical research and his fundamental belief in its worth and utility never seemed to flag, from the mid-1940s to the mid-1960s. He wanted to know who was involved at every stage of the fort's history. If he anticipated complete personnel records, and it appears that he did, he was deeply disappointed. His inquiry in the summer of 1963 at the Public Archives of Canada (PAC) — now the National Archives of Canada (NAC) — did elicit the names of a few people. J.D. Herbert, head of the PAC, found evidence of the presence of Captain Peter Drummond in 1798 when the British formally purchased St. Joseph Island. Herbert conceded that any information at the PAC was fragmentary, but he excused this on the ground that the fort was really peripheral, even at the moment of the famous raid against Mackinac. Smith, of course, disagreed. He believed that the fort, tiny and isolated though it was, was critical in the preservation of Canada in 1812.[25]

Yet, despite Herbert's protestation that the fort lacked importance, Parks Canada nevertheless decided to develop the site into a historic park. The campaign by Smith and his supporters began to bear real fruit in the 1960s. By then John Diefenbaker, a Progressive Conservative, had become prime minister, and Smith appealed to Henry Lang of the Progressive Conservative Association in Sault Ste. Marie. On behalf of both the Legion Branch and the Chamber of Commerce from St. Joseph Island, Smith repeated his earlier arguments: local and national pride, lack of patriotism in the schools, economic development. He urged Lang to use his influence with Walter Dinsdale, Conservative MP for Brandon-Souris and Diefenbaker's Minister of Northern Affairs and Natural Resources. He also noted the Diefenbaker government's decision to revive Louisbourg as a historic attraction and suggested that what it was doing on Cape Breton Island it might do on St. Joseph Island as well. Smith said:

> In those years [1812–1814], Canada first learned to stand on its own feet, and no place in Canada has a better claim to recognition in this conflict than Fort St. Joseph.[26]

Lang forwarded the message to Dinsdale, and Northern Affairs sent an engineer to consider Smith's arguments: (1) that there should be a survey of the fort's original boundaries; (2) that the blockhouse should be rehabilitated; (3) that the army cemetery should be restored; (4) that the fort occupied one of the few public access points to the shoreline of St. Joseph Island, a place popular with weekend visitors; (5) that revival of the fort would stimulate the local economy.[27]

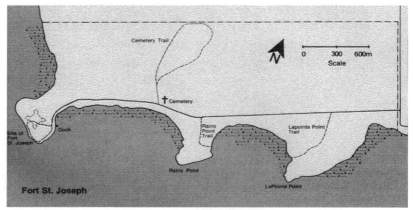

Many supporters and historians hope that the army cemetery will be restored, and the ruins of Fort St. Joseph revived as a tourist attraction.

Archaeologists from the University of Toronto followed in the summer of 1963, when Lester Pearson, MP for Algoma East, replaced Diefenbaker as prime minister. The new Liberal government pursued the Fort St. Joseph project that Diefenbaker had authorized. That year, the archaeologists compiled a photographic record of any standing masonry: walls, gates, the guardhouse, half the blockhouse, and other buildings. They found the first bake house and partially uncovered a second building.

In 1964, Professor Michael Ashworth and fifteen of his students mounted a second expedition. Their task was not light. The fire of 1814 had been destructive. A layer of topsoil had accumulated since then. Somebody had dumped boulders onto the site in 1947. In 1948, a bulldozer had removed archaeological evidence of the northwesterly chimney.[28] The amount of limestone remaining on the site in 1963–1964 was insufficient to account for the amount of construction that would have been required. However, with skill, imagination, and determination, Ashworth and his students persevered. Subsequently Elizabeth Vincent produced her admirable report on the fort's history, and Stephen Cumbaa the fascinating analysis of the edibles that sustained the fort community. On the basis of what they and others dug and discovered, Parks Canada was able to develop the site into a tourist attraction by 1978.

Conclusions

On 16 July 1812, prehistoric events (Aboriginal migrations), European history (Anglo-French strife), and United States politics converged at Fort St. Joseph: without the Aboriginals, the outcome would have been different; without centuries of conflict between Great Britain and France, there might not have been military outposts in the Upper Great Lakes region; and without political pressure upon President James Madison in Washington, there might not have been a declaration of war in 1812, nor might there ever have been such a declaration, as with the collapse of Napoleon that began that very year, Congress might soon have considered war unnecessary. As it was, the British *did* withdraw their offending orders-in-council *before* the US declaration of war, but *not before* Congress became aware of the withdrawal. With the return of peace to Europe, differences between Great Britain and the United States would have become, once again, academic, hardly worth fighting over. A fort on

St. Joseph Island, let alone one whose garrison played a decisive role in the War of 1812, was far from inevitable.

Yet Fort St. Joseph has consistently represented a reluctant investment that governments and the private sector hesitated to support. Lord Dorchester thought there were better uses for his military budget, and his successors put the minimum of money and military personnel into it. Fur traders regarded Mackinac Island, Montreal, and Hudson Bay as more critical centres of activity. As the expedition of 16 July 1812 sailed away to victory, it also signed the death warrant for the island, which it left unprotected. When the War of 1812 ended, Great Britain and the United States remained adversaries at least until 1871, arguably until the 1890s, and the British Army and Navy established bases across what is now Canada from Halifax to Esquimalt. British authorities were not, however, willing to re-invest in Fort St. Joseph.

Thanks to the efforts of Glyn Smith and his collaborators, Parks Canada, and various levels of government, Fort St. Joseph experienced a twentieth-century resurrection — but barely. Parks Canada has poured money into Fort Louisbourg on Cape Breton Island, thereby creating a site that for decades tens of thousands of tourists have travelled thousands of kilometres to see. Fort Beauséjour and Fort George, with their restored buildings, are tourist magnets for those who travel the Trans-Canada Highway between New Brunswick and Nova Scotia or who visit the Niagara Peninsula. The private sector has rendered Mackinac Island one of the most delightful vacation spots in the United States — a haven free of vehicular traffic, where cyclists, joggers, rollerbladers, and horseback riders can exercise, visit historic sites, dine in gourmet restaurants, and live in luxurious hotels. Meanwhile, Fort St. Joseph languishes, as it did for most of its brief life, on the periphery, unknown or forgotten. There is a museum that vividly recreates the past. The foundations of its buildings permit the imaginative to envisage an earlier zone of conflict in a highly picturesque setting. The cemetery serves as a reminder that Fort St. Joseph represented more than a prolonged camping experience for the young. That is all.

There are reasons for this. No government poured money into the original Fort St. Joseph the way the government of King Louis XV invested in Louisbourg. Unlike Fort Beauséjour, Fort St. Joseph does not sit beside the Trans-Canada Highway. It is not as close to population centres as Fort George or Fort Mackinac.

It would appear that few, except Glyn Smith and his closest collaborators, have realized the enormous tourist potential of Fort St. Joseph. This should change. As the new millenium begins, the Canadian dollar sits well below its US counterpart in value. Canadians, therefore, seek vacation destinations inside Canada, and Americans, wanting good value for their money, often consider crossing the border into Canada, where *their* money has exceptional purchasing power. As Canada decentralizes and provinces assume increasing responsibility for tourism, residents of Ontario may look increasingly for destinations within their own province rather than for destinations in Nova Scotia or New Brunswick. With global warming, Fort St. Joseph may appear more attractive in summer than Fort George. Above all, millions of travellers pass along Highway 17 each year within an hour's drive of Fort St. Joseph.

Imagine what a co-ordinated effort by government and the private sector might do! Parks Canada could restore some of the buildings and put furnishings from the period inside them so that visitors could see more than mere foundations. The Ontario government could promote Fort St. Joseph, even if it is a federal responsibility, in its tourist literature and promote it on signs along Highway 17. Either level of government could offer seed money, as in Charlottetown or Dawson City, to hire a few actors and musicians. With the help of amateur volunteers, presumably residents of St. Joseph Island, there could be skits about the prehistoric and historic past. Musicians could offer summer concerts amid the ruins, perhaps but not necessarily with tunes from the years 1796–1812. How many might travel to such a setting for a rendition of "The 1812 Overture"?

The upsurge in tourism would stimulate the island's private sector. Some visitors would stay in campsites and patronize grocery stores and souvenir shops. Some would prefer motels and restaurants. All would buy gasoline, if not on the island itself then in nearby service stations. Even then, some paved roads could be restricted to non-motorized and local traffic. The very thought of cycling, jogging, or rollerblading in such an environment would attract additional people, whose money would also enrich the island's economy. St. Joseph Island could offer an unusual combination of historic tourism, eco-tourism (at the bird sanctuary next to the fort) and outdoor activity.

Some prefer Fort St. Joseph as a collection of broken foundations in an authentic location. This, they feel, is closer to the historic reality than any reconstruction project along the lines of Louisbourg, Fort Beauséjour, or Fort George could possibly be. Nevertheless, reconstruction need not be incompatible with historic integrity. Indeed, it may be a great teacher. In order to lure tourists to a remote corner of Newfoundland, L'Anse aux Meadows — site of a Viking settlement almost one thousand years ago — Parks Canada has erected three buildings of the period so that visitors can see the way the Vikings lived. The buildings are *adjacent to*, a few metres removed from, the actual site where Thorfinn Karlsefni and his Greenlandic colonists actually lived. This satisfies both those who want to leave the authentic archaeological record totally undisturbed, and those who want to see something and to take interesting pictures after the long drive to L'Anse aux Meadows. Similarly, despite the elaborate restoration process at Louisbourg and the many photo opportunities for those who go there, more than half the original site remains undisturbed (except by nature) the way it was in the

A Viking-era building erected by Parks Canada immediately adjacent to the site at L'Anse aux Meadows, Newfoundland, settled by Vikings one thousand years ago.
Photo by Graeme S. Mount, 1987

Mounds indicate the actual site of the Viking settlement at L'Anse aux Meadows, Newfoundland, c. A.D. 1000.
Photo of his son Andrew by Graeme S. Mount, 1987

eighteenth century. Future archaeologists will be able to work there, unencumbered by mistakes their twentieth-century predecessors might have made.

The rest of the world certainly improves upon the relics spared by nature. Hadrian's Wall, erected across the north of England early in the second century as a barrier against the wild people from what is now Scotland, almost disappeared after the fall of the Roman Empire in the fifth century. Those who lived in early mediaeval England had a higher priority than the purity of the historic record: survival itself. Accordingly, they helped themselves to rocks from Hadrian's Wall in order to build homes and roads. Without reconstruction and restoration, directed by skilled historians and archaeologists in the twentieth century, there would not be much to see. Residents of Northumberlandshire have gained economically from the influx of tourists who want to walk upon a portion of Hadrian's Wall, and tourists spend money there and delight in the experience.

What the British have done in terms of restoration, other history-conscious, tourist-conscious people in Europe, Asia,

The restored portions of Hadrian's Wall, near Chester, attract tourists to Northumberlandshire in northernmost England. With a minimum of imagination, visitors can envisage the centuries when Roman soldiers stood on guard against the Picts to the north.
Photo by Graeme S. Mount, 1986

The government of Guatemala and archaeologists from the United States have uncovered part of the Mayan city of Tikal, which flourished from the third to the ninth centuries. Pictures demonstrate the difference between Temples 1 and 2, uncovered and restored, and Temple 3, still hidden by verdure.
Photo by Graeme S. Mount, 1977

The People's Republic of China had no hesitation about restoring sections of the Great Wall. Here tourists and merchants take advantage of the restored Badaling Section near Beijing.
Photo by Graeme S. Mount, 1999

The Republic of Korea (South Korea) has restored Seoul's Ch'angdokgung Palace, first built in the fifteenth century, as a tourist attraction.
Photo by Graeme S. Mount, 1999

The Roman emperor Augustus, mentioned in the New Testament, erected a monument at what is now La Turbie, France, to celebrate his military victories. French authorities have partially restored the monument.
Photo by Graeme S. Mount, 1990

and Latin America have also done. Nobody who has seen the restored monument at La Turbie, France, first erected by the Roman Emperor Augustus to celebrate his military victories in the area, can fail to appreciate the hardships of the workers or the emperor's vanity. Those who travelled to see a mere pile of rubble would find it forgettable. China's Qing dynasty (1644–1911) had invaded China from Manchuria by bribing guards along the Great Wall of China, which their Ming predecessors (1368–1644), had restored. Under the circumstances the Qing had little confidence in the wall and allowed it to deteriorate. In recent decades, leaders of the People's Republic of China, well aware of the tourist potential and historical significance of that wall, have invested heavily in the reconstruction of some of the most scenic portions. Again, visitors can appreciate its enormity and the challenge to those who built and use it in a way that would otherwise have been impossible. Ch'angdokgung Palace in Seoul, South Korea, whose construction began in 1405, is a photographer's delight. Its buildings and gardens enrapture all except the extremely dull in spirit. Nobody suggests that it should remain as it was after decades of Japanese occupation and the destruction of the Korean War (1950–1953). Mexicans have made the most of archaeological sites on the plateau near Mexico City and on the coastal lowlands of Yucatan, and their economy has benefitted accordingly. Neighbouring Guatemala, Belize, and Honduras realize that if they want tourists to see *their* Mayan wonders, they must compete. Few except professional archaeologists will travel long distances to see undisturbed, or almost undisturbed, ruins.

It is to be hoped that governments in Ottawa and Queen's Park, the business community, and residents of St. Joseph Island itself see and grasp the existing opportunities. It may seem presumptuous, even foolish, to compare Fort St. Joseph with L'Anse aux Meadows or Louisbourg, let alone Hadrian's Wall and the Great Wall of China. Yet, consider the context. It is the oldest historic attraction within a radius of hundreds of kilometres on the Canadian side of the border. It sits in an area of scenic beauty and fresh air. It is accessible. Glyn Smith was right. Canadians ought to grasp opportunities that exist and exploit them in a positive way.

An Alternative Vision

Glyn Smith, one surmises, would be pleased but scarcely satisfied. Delineation, he might fume, is no substitute for restoration. Almost certainly he would favour the case for restoration eloquently argued in the conclusion of this book. Yet some, including one of this volume's authors, would quietly suggest that the site, with its features sketched mysteriously in tracings of stone and soft depressions on the earth, should remain as is. Money that would otherwise go into restoration might better be spent on interpretation. In an age and on a continent cluttered with historical stage sets, a few places should be left to work their osmotic alchemy slowly on mind and spirit. In its own way, and its own environment, Fort St. Joseph is the equivalent of another gem in the national parks system. Grasslands, tucked into the virtually vacant, short-grass prairie of southwestern Saskatchewan, offers no restorations and few restrictions. For the reflective wanderer the opportunity to stand within a teepee ring and gather the valley of the Frenchman River into the mind's eye, is to imagine the buffalo-centred world of Aboriginal America. That same dreamer, standing on the grassy knoll, within the foundations of the old fort, gathering within that same mind's eye the waters of the North Channel and the St. Mary's River, Drummond Island, and Detour Passage, enters the world described in these pages.

Notes

INTRODUCTION

1. Pierre Berton, *The Invasion of Canada* (Toronto: McClelland and Stewart, 1980), pp. 90–101.

PROLOGUE

1. P.F. Karrow, *Quarternary Geology, St. Joseph Island* (Toronto: Ministry of Northern Development and Mines, Ontario Geological Survey, Open File Report 5809, 1991), p. 63.

2. Karrow, pp. 55, 66.

3. Karrow, pp. 67–68. See also Marginal Notes, Ontario Geological Survey, Map p. 2581, Geological Series-

Preliminary Map, Quarternary Geology of St. Joseph
Island, Algoma District, included in Karrow, pp. 5–6.

4. Edward S. Rogers and Donald Smith, *Aboriginal
   Ontario: Historical Perspectives on the First Nations*
   (Toronto: Dundurn, 1994), p. 24.

5. R. Cole Harris (ed.) and Geoffrey J. Matthews
   (cartographer/designer), *Historical Atlas of Canada*
   (Toronto: University of Toronto Press, 1987), vol. I,
   plates 1–5. For an overview, see Chris J. Ellis and D.
   Brian Deller, "Paleo-Indians," in Chris J. Ellis and Neal
   Ferris (eds.), *The Archaeology of Southern Ontario to
   A.D. 1650* (London, Ontario: Occasional Publications of
   the London Chapter, Ontario Archaeological Society,
   Publication No. 5, 1990), p. 38.

6. Ellis and Ferris, *passim*.

7. Harris and Matthews, plates 6 and 7.

8. Harris and Matthews, plate 12.

9. Charles E. Cleland, *The Prehistoric Animal Ecology and
   Ethnozoology of the Upper Great Lakes Region* (Ann
   Arbor: University of Michigan Press, Anthropological
   Papers, Museum of Anthropology, No. 29, 1966), pp.
   4–7, 33–35, 89–90.

10. Fort St. Joseph, National Historic Site, Management
    Plan, Public Open House, 16 June 1998, Canadian
    Heritage, Parks Canada, p. 3.

11. Stephen L. Cumbaa, *A Study of Military and Civilian Food
    Remains from Fort St. Joseph, Ontario (1795–1828)*
    (Ottawa: Zooarchaeological Identification Centre, National
    Museum of Natural Sciences, 31 March 1979), pp. 25–28.

12. Richard Asa Yarnell, *Aboriginal Relationships Between Culture and Plant Life in the Great Lakes Region*, (Ann Arbor: University of Michigan Press, Anthropological Papers, Museum of Anthropology, No. 23, 1964), p. 12.

13. Susan Rapalje Martin, "A Reconsideration of Aboriginal Fishing Strategies in the Northern Great Lakes Region," *American Antiquity*, LIV, 3 (1989), p. 596.

14. See James E. Fitting, *The Archaeology of Michigan: A Guide to the Prehistory of the Great Lakes Region* (Bloomfield Hills, Michigan: Cranbrook Institute of Science, 1975), especially Chapter VII, "Those who were there", pp. 192–199.

15. *Dictionary of Canadian Biography, 1000–1700* (Toronto: University of Toronto Press), vol. I, pp. 248–249.

16. Margaret G. Hanna and Brian Kooyman, *Approaches to Algonquian History* (Calgary: University of Calgary Archaeological Association, 1982), p. 260; Yarnell, p. 15.

CHAPTER I

1. William Ferguson, *Scotland's Relations with England: A Survey to 1707* (Edinburgh: John Donald, 1977), p.197– 253

2. For background on the background of Fort Michilimackinac, see Bruce Catton, *Michigan: A Bicentennial History* (New York: W.W. Norton, 1976), p. 26.

3. Robert S. Allen, *A History of the British Indian Department in North America (1755–1830)*, (Ottawa: Department of Indian Affairs and Northern Development,

Manuscript Report Number 109, December 1971), pp. 18–19.

4. The quotation comes from Catton, p. 47. For the entire background to the massacre, see Catton, pp. 39–57; Willis F. Dunbar, *Michigan: A History of the Wolverine State* (Grand Rapids: Eerdmans, 1965), pp. 64–71; Calvin Goodrich, *The First Michigan Frontier* (Ann Arbor: University of Michigan Press, 1940), pp. 268–273.

5. David A. Armour (ed.), *Massacre at Mackinac: Alexander Henry's Travels and Adventures in Canada and the Indian Territories between the Years 1760 and 1764* (Mackinac Island: Mackinac Island State Park Commission, 1966), pp. 43–60. The quotation comes from p. 49.

6. Allen, p. 27.

7. Allen, p. 35.

8. Allen, pp. 46–47.

9. Allen, p. 55.

10. A.L. Burt, *The United States, Great Britain, and British North America* (Toronto: Ryerson, 1966 [1940]), pp. 138–139, 158; S.F. Bemis, *Jay's Treaty: A Study in Commerce and Diplomacy* (New York: Macmillan, 1924 [1923].

11. Elizabeth Vincent, *Fort St. Joseph: A History* (Ottawa: Parks Canada, 1978), p. 64.

12. Graeme S. Mount, John Abbott, Michael J. Mulloy, *The Border at Sault Ste. Marie* (Toronto: Dundurn Press, 1995).

13. Glyn Smith Collection, "Old Days and a New Day for St. Joseph's Island," Speech of December 1951, MG5, Series 1, Box 3, File 2, Sault Ste. Marie (Ontario) Public Library. Cited hereafter as Glyn Smith Collection, SSMPL.

14. Quoted in Joseph and Estelle Bayliss, *Historic St. Joseph Island* (Cedar Rapids, Iowa: Torch Press, 1938), p. 22.

CHAPTER II

1. Elizabeth Vincent, *Fort St. Joseph: A History* (Ottawa: Parks Canada, 1978), pp. 65–66.

2. For a comprehensive review of the construction process at Fort St. Joseph, see Vincent, pp. 78–95.

3. Colonel George Landmann, *Adventures and Recollections of Colonel Landmann* (London: Colburn and Company, 1852), two volumes, vol. I, pp. 316–317.

4. *Ibid.*, p. 314.

5. *Ibid.*, p. 290.

6. Vincent, p. 89.

7. Vincent, pp. 98–99.

8. Vincent, pp. 92–95. See also, Joseph and Estelle Bayliss, *Historic St. Joseph Island* (Cedar Rapids, Iowa: The Torch Press, 1938), pp. 36–38; this source provides a list of civilians who built at the fort.

9. Ellen R. Lee, "A Research Model for Extracting Interactive Patterns at a Fur Trade Post on the Upper Great Lakes: Fort St. Joseph, Ontario, 1796–1829," MA

Thesis, University of Manitoba, 1986, p. 6.

CHAPTER III

1. Mary Quayle Innis (ed.), *Mrs. Simcoe's Diary* (New York: St. Martin Press, 1965), p. 126. For other examples of war scares, see pp. 123 (15 May 1794) and 134 (29 Aug. 1794).

2. Patrick C.T. White, *A Nation on Trial: America and the War of 1812* (New York: Wiley, 1965), 14–16.

3. Harry L. Coles, *The War of 1812* (Chicago: University of Chicago Press, 1965), p. 7.

4. *Montreal Gazette*, 10 Aug. 1807.

5. *Montreal Gazette*, 17 Aug. 1807.

6. Reprinted in Ruhl Bartlett, *The Record of American Diplomacy* (New York: Knopf, 1964), p. 143.

7. White, p. 63.

8. Books on the causes of the War of 1812 include Harry L. Coles, *The War of 1812* (Chicago: University of Chicago Press, 1965); Bradford Perkins, ed., *The Causes of the War of 1812: National Honor or National Interest?* (New York: Holt, Rinehart and Winston, 1962); White; J.C.A. Stagg, *Mr. Madison's War* (Princeton: Princeton University Press, 1983), chapter 1. See also Donald R. Hickey, "Federalist Party Unity and the War of 1812," *Journal of American Studies*, XII, 1 (April 1978), pp. 23–39; and Reginald Horsman, "On to Canada: Manifest Destiny and United States Strategy in the War of 1812," *Michigan Historical Review*, XIII, 2 (Fall 1987), pp. 1–24.

9. C.P. Stacey, *The Undefended Border: The Myth and The Reality* (Ottawa: Canadian Historical Association, No.1: 1953).

10. Allen, pp. 230–231.

CHAPTER IV

1. The substance is from the *Wisconsin Historical Collections,* XVII, pp. 439–440, conveyed to Glyn Smith in a Memo from the Public Archives of Canada, 25 July 1961, Box 3, Series 1, File 1, Glyn Smith Collection.

2. Bayliss, p. 64.

3. The estimate of 1,500 miles from Quebec City to Fort St. Joseph is that of Governor-in-Chief Sir George Prevost to the British Prime Minister, the Earl of Liverpool, 18 May 1812; *Michigan Pioneer and Historical Collections* (Lansing: Darius D. Thorp, State Printer and Binder, 1889), XV, p. 87.

4. Alex Campbell, n.p., to Duke of Kent, Quebec City (?), 1800, *Michigan Pioneer and Historical Collections*, XV (Lansing: Darius D. Thorp, State Printer, 1889), p. 16. The estimate of 322 miles originated with a report of Lieutenant Colonel Ralph Bruyeres, written in Quebec City 24 Aug. 1811; *ibid.*, p. 54.

5. Bayliss, pp. 41–42.

6. Ellen R. Lee, "A Research Model for Extracting Interactive Patterns at a Fur Trade Post on the Upper Great Lakes: Fort St. Joseph, 1796–1829," M.A. thesis, University of Manitoba.

7. *Ibid.*, pp. 43–50.

8. Elizabeth Vincent, *Fort St. Joseph: A History* (Ottawa: Parks Canada, 1978), p. 159.

9. Ron Whate, "Frontier-Post Pearlware: Ceramics recovered at the 'Siberia of the North,'" *National Parks Centennial* (July–Aug. 1985), pp. 37–41.

10. The Commanding Officer, Fort St. Joseph, to Lieutenant Green, Military Secretary, n.p., 8 May and 9 July 1805, R.G. 8, C Series, vol. 923, reel C-3279, pp. 51–52 and 216, NAC. See also Dennis Carter-Edwards, *The 41st (the Welsh) Regiment 1700–1815* (Ottawa: Parks Canada, 1986), p. 14. While Carter-Edwards was describing an incident at Fort George, members of that same Welch Regiment had a tour of duty at Fort St. Joseph.

11. *Ibid.*, pp. 164–165.

12. Vincent, pp. 7–8.

13. Correspondence on the Duggan affair can be found in the *Michigan Pioneer and Historical Society* (Lansing: Robert Smith and Company, State Printers and Binders, 1895), XXIII, pp. 6–13. See also Bayliss, pp. 36, 38, 44.

14. Lieutenant Robert Cowell, Fort St. Joseph, to Major James Green, 25 July 1892, *Michigan Pioneer and Historical Society*, XXIII, p. 17.

15. George Landmann, *Adventures and Recollections of Colonel Landmann* (London:Colburn and Company, 1852), I, p. 317.

16. *Ibid.*, p. 318.

17. *Ibid.*, p. 91.

18. *Ibid.*, p. 92.

19. *Ibid.*, pp. 93–94.

20. *Ibid.*, p. 90.

21. Letter from Dr. Richardson, Fort St. Joseph, to John Askin, Senior, 6 Aug. 1801, in M.M. Quayle (ed.), *The John Askin Papers, 1796–1820*, vol. II (Detroit: The Burton Historical Collection, 1931), p. 356. Cited hereafter as Askin Letters.

22. Richardson, Fort St. Joseph, to Askin, Senior, Detroit, 9 Feb. 1802, p. 368, Askin Letters.

23. Askin Junior, Fort St. Joseph, to Askin Senior, presumably Amherstburg or Detroit, 4 July 1807, Askin Letters.

24. Askin Junior, Fort St. Joseph, to Askin Senior, presumably Amherstburg or Detroit, 10 Aug. 1807, p. 554, Askin Letters.

25. Joseph and Estelle Bayliss, *Historic Fort St. Joseph Island* (Cedar Rapids, Iowa: The Torch Press, 1938), p. 52.

CHAPTER V

1. Among the most comprehensive accounts of the fighting along the frontier between Upper Canada and the United States must be those of G.F.G. Stanley, C.P. Stacey, and Pierre Berton. See G.F.G. Stanley, "The Indians in the War of 1812," *Canadian Historical Review*, XXXI (1950), pp. 145–165; "The Significance of Six Nations Participation in the War of 1812," *Ontario History*, LV (1963), pp.

213–231; *The War of 1812: Land Operations* (Toronto: Macmillan, 1983). See also C.P. Stacey, "Upper Canada at War, 1814: Captain Armstrong Reports," *Ontario History*, XLVIII (1956), pp. 37–42; and "The War of 1812 in Canadian History," *Ontario History*, L (1958), pp. 153–159. See also Pierre Berton, *The Invasion of Canada*, 1812–1813 (Toronto: McClelland and Stewart, 1980); and *Flames Across the Border*, 1814 (Toronto: McClelland and Stewart, 1981). See also Robert S. Allen, "His Majesty's Indian Allies: Native Peoples, the British Crown and the War of 1812," *Michigan Historical Review*, XIV, 2 (Fall 1988), pp. 1–14; Gerry T. Altoff, "Oliver Hazard Perry and the Battle of Lake Erie," *Michigan Historical Review*, XIV, 2 (Fall, 1988), pp. 25–57; Dennis Carter-Edwards, "The War of 1812 Along the Detroit Frontier: A Canadian Perspective," *Michigan Historical Review*, XIII, 2 (Fall 1987), pp. 25–50.

2. Alex Campbell, n.p. to Duke of Kent, Quebec City (?), 1800, in *Michigan Pioneer and Historical Collections*, XV (Lansing: Larius D. Thorp, State Printer, 1889), pp. 12 and 18.

3. Vincent, pp. 4–7, 16, 23.

4. A. Gray, Montreal, to Sir George Prevost, Quebec City, 13 Jan. 1812, *Michigan Pioneer and Historical Collections*, XV, p. 71.

5. Taken from a sign at Fort Mackinac, Mackinac Island, 5 June 1998. Sources of information about Fort Mackinac during the period of British occupation (1780–1796) and at the time of the attack in 1812 include signs around the fort, which has become a tourist attraction, and various books, most notably: Kathryne Belden Ashley, *Islands of the Manitou* (Sault Ste. Marie, Mich.: Lake Superior State College, n.d.), pp. 26–39; J.P. Barry, Sentinels in the

Wilderness (Lansing, Mich.: Thunder Bay Press, c. 1994), pp. 60–62; William F. Coffin, *1812: The War and its Moral: A Canadian Chronicle* (Montreal: John Lovell, 1864), pp. 44–47; Catton, pp. 62–63; Dunbar, pp. 125–127; Brian Leigh Dunnigan, *King's Men at Mackinac: The British Garrisons, 1780–1796* (Mackinac Island: State Park Commission, 1973); George N. Fuller, *Michigan: A Centennial History of the State and its People* (two volumes), I (Chicago: Lewis, 1939), pp. 125, 136; Fred C. Hamil, "Michigan in the War of 1812," *Michigan History*, XLIV, 3 (Sept. 1960), pp. 260–269; M.O. Hammond, *Canadian Footprints* (Toronto: Macmillan, 1926), pp. 180–183; James Hannay, *History of the War of 1812* (Toronto: Morang & Co., 1905), pp. 32–35, 300–307; Walter Havighurst, *Three Flags at the Straits: The Forts of Mackinac* (Englewood Cliffs, N.J.: Prentice Hall, 1966), pp. 90–128; Hinsperger, *Stories of the Past: 300 Years of Soo History* (n.p. 1967), pp. 16–17; George S. May, *War 1812* (Mackinac Island: State Park Commission); Eugene T. Petersen, *Mackinac Island: Its History in Pictures* (Mackinac Island: Mackinac Island State Park Commission, 1973), pp. 12–14; James Strang, *Ancient and Modern Michilimackinac;* W.P. Strickland, *Old Mackinac: The Fortress of the Lakes and its Surroundings* (Philadelphia: James Challen & Son, 1860), pp. 100–104; J.A. Van Fleet, *Old and New Mackinac* (Cincinnati: Western Methodist Book Concern, 1874), pp. 97–120; Keith R. Widder, *Reveillé Till Taps: Soldier Life at Fort Mackinac, 1780–1895* (Mackinac Island: State Park Commission, 1972), pp. 1–35; Meade C. Williams, *Early Mackinac: An Historical and Descriptive Sketch* (St. Louis: Buschart Bros. Print, 1903), pp. 56–76.

6. L. Oughtred Woltz, "The Chippewa Cession of Mackinac to George III, May 12, 1781," *Michigan History*, IX, 2 (April 1925), pp. 136–142.

7. For a full account of Jay's Treaty, see Samuel Flagg Bemis, *Jay's Treaty: A Study in Commerce and Diplomacy* (New York: Macmillan, 1924).

8. Pierre Berton, *The Invasion of Canada, 1812–1813* (Toronto: McClelland and Stewart, 1980), p. 101.

9. Van Fleet, p. 98.

10. Vincent, p. 8.

11. For further information about the role of Dickson, see the letter which Roberts sent to Brock 12 July 1812; Roberts, Fort St. Joseph, to Brock, York, 12 July 1812, RG 8 I "C" Series, National Archives of Canada (NAC), Ottawa. Cited hereafter as RG 8 I "C".

12. Askin, Mackinac, to William Cluies, Fort George, 18 July 1812, RG 8 I "C".

13. May, p. 11.

14. Roberts, Mackinac, to the Adjutant General, 17 July 1812; also, Roberts, Mackinac, to Brock, York, 17 July; both in RG 8 I "C" Series.

15. William Puthuff, Washington, to Lewis Cass, Michigan, Michilimackinac Agency, 14 May 1816, conveyed to Glyn Smith in a Memo from the Public Archives of Canada, 25 July 1961, Box 3, Series 1, File 1, Glyn Smith Collection, SSMPL.

16. William Maher Howell, "The Arrival of Dobbins at Erie," *Inland Seas,* LI, 2 (Summer 1995), pp. 32–34.

17. Roberts praised his civilian allies; Roberts, Mackinac, to Brock, York, 17 July 1812, RG 8 I "C".

18. Quoted on a sign inside Fort Mackinac, 5 June 1998.

19. Askin, Mackinac, to William Cluies, Fort George, 18 July 1812, RG 8 I "C".

20. Van Fleet, pp. 102–103. The quotation comes from p. 102. Correspondence of such participants at the outbreak of hostilities and the capture of Fort Mackinac as Roberts, Dickson, and Pothier is available in *Michigan Pioneer and Historical Collections*, XV, pp. 101–109, 141–144.

21. Hanks, Mackinac, to Hull, Detroit, 12 August 1812, reprinted in Williams, p. 59.

22. Hanks to Hull, 12 Aug. 1812, Williams, p. 61.

23. For an account of the War of 1812 in 1814, see Pierre Berton, *Flames Across the Border* (Toronto: McClelland and Stewart, 1981).

24. Allen, p. 189–190.

25. Graeme S. Mount, John Abbott, Michael J. Mulloy, *The Border at Sault Ste. Marie* (Toronto: Dundurn, 1995), pp. 5–6.

26. Smith's notes, no date; Box 3, MG 5, Series 1, File 2, Glyn Smith Collection, Sault Ste. Marie Public Library, SSMPL.

27. Van Fleet, p. 110.

28. George Sheppard, *Plunder, Profit, and Paroles: A Social History of the War of 1812 in Upper Canada* (Montreal: McGill-Queen's University Press, 1994).

29. May, pp. 19–20.

30. This information about Assigniach is taken from signs at the site of the former British army base at Penetanguishene, which the Ontario government has restored as a tourist attraction.

31. Bob Malcomson, "War on the Lakes," *The Beaver* (April/May 1990), pp. 44–52.

32. Washington report of 18 June, included in the 6 July 1812 issue of the *Montreal Gazette*.

33. *Boston Sentinel*, 20 May 1812, reprinted in *Montreal Gazette*, 8 June 1812.

34. For further information about the Battle of Lake Erie, see Phoebe-May Bowen, "The Battle of Lake Erie in the War of 1812," *Inland Seas*, XLIII, 3 (Fall, 1987), pp. 178–187.

35. From letter book of Ramsay Crooks in Burton Library, Detroit, 21 Aug. 1814, conveyed to Glyn Smith in a Memo from the Public Archives of Canada, 25 July 1961, Box 3, Series 1, File 1, Glyn Smith Collection.

36. Boucherville to Prevost, 13 June 1812, *Michigan Pioneer and Historical Collections*, XV, p. 81.

37. May, p. 21.

38. May, 21–22.

39. May, p. 26.

40. An extract from an account of the debate in the House of Commons, 11 April 1815, reprinted in Ruhl Bartlett,

The Record of American Diplomacy (New York: Knopf, 1964), p. 153.

41. US Congress, *Debates and Proceedings*, Thirteenth Congress—Third Session, 18 Feb. 1815, pp. 255–256.

CHAPTER VI

1. Vincent, pp. 225–235.

2. W. McGillivray of the North West Company, Montreal, to Secretary Lt. Col. Foster, Quebec City, 16 Oct. 1815, *Michigan Pioneer and Historical Society* (Lansing: Wynkorp Hallenbeck Crawford Co.: State Printers, 1910), vol. XVI, p. 351.

3. McDouall, Mackinac, to Foster, Quebec City, 15 May 1815, *Michigan Pioneer and Historical Society* vol. XVI, p. 105.

4. McDouall, Mackinac, to Lt. Gen. Sir George Murray, Quebec City, 17 May 1815, *Michigan Pioneer and Historical Society*, XVI, p. 109.

5. McDouall, Drummond Island, to Foster, Quebec City, 25 Feb. 1816, *Michigan Pioneer and Historical Society*, XVI, pp. 430–431.

6. See the correspondence of McDouall to authorities in Quebec City, 15–17 May 1815; *Michigan Pioneer and Historical Society*, XVI, pp. 90–111.

7. Vincent, p. 235; David Wingfield, "Four Years on the Lakes of Canada," p. 57.

8. Vincent, p. 236.

9. Vincent, pp. 237–238.

10. Vincent, pp. 240–241.

11. Vincent, p. 246.

12. Vincent, pp. 246–248. Portlock's report is undated.

13. Report of J.E. Portlock, Lieutenant in the Royal Engineers, "Memorandum respecting the new works & projected Improvements as proposed for the Canadas for Major General Sir James Carmichael Smith, 31 March 1826," *Michigan Pioneer and Historical Collections*, XXIII (1893), p. 413. Cited in Glyn Smith Collection.

14. Vincent, pp. 251, 254.

15. The most thorough account — although a passionately American one, almost to the point of chauvinism — of the British military presence on Drummond Island is that by Samuel F. Cook, *Drummond Island: The Story of the British Occupation, 1815–1828* (Lansing, Mich.: Author's edition, 1896). The quotation comes from p. 6. See also Ashley, pp. 40–81. For an account of British relations with the Indians, see Colin G. Calloway, "The End of an Era: British-Indian Relations in the Great Lakes Region after the War of 1812," *Michigan Historical Review*, XII, 2 (Fall, 1986), pp. 1–20.

16. McDouall, Drummond Island, to Foster, Quebec City, 29 Oct. 1815, *Michigan Pioneer and Historical Society*, XVI, pp. 372–373.

17. Cook, p. 82.

18. Cook, pp. 10–11.

19. Cook, p. 13.

20. Cook, pp. 13–22.

21. Major G. Henderson, Quebec City, to Lieutenant Portlock, Royal Engineer, Drummond Island, 1 March 1817; *Michigan Pioneer and Historical Society*, XVI, pp. 570–571; J. Hale, Deputy Paymaster, Quebec City, to Lieutenant Colonel Addison, Militry Secretary, 12 March 1817, *ibid.*, pp. 572–573; Lieutenant Colonel E.W. Dumford, Quebec City, to Lieutenant Colonel Harvey, Deputy Adjutant General, 22 Aug. 1818, *ibid.*, pp. 634–635.

22. J.E. Portlock, Report of the State of the Posts of Amherstburg, Drummond Island, and St. Josephs, n.d., *Michigan Pioneer and Historical Society*, XXIII, pp. 411–413. Cited hereafter as Portlock Report.

23. Portlock Report, p. 413.

24. Major Thomas Howard, Drummond Island, to Foster, Quebec City, 12 Aug. 1818, *Michigan Pioneer and Historical Society*, XVI, pp. 630–631.

25. Dunbar, p. 137.

26. Cook, pp. 75–76. See also Barry, pp. 136–137.

27. Vincent, pp. 255–261.

28. Cook, p. 82.

CHAPTER VII

1. Vincent, pp. 255–265.

2. Vincent, pp. 265–271.

3. S.A. Wallace, Windsor, to Smith, St. Joseph Island, 4 Aug. 1949; Box 3, MG 5, Series 1, File 1, Glyn Smith Collection, SSMPL.

4. Wallace to Smith, 13 Oct. 1949; Box 3, MG 5, Series 1, File 1, SSMPL.

5. Derrer to Smith, 10 Nov. 1948; Box 3, MG 5, Series 2, File 1.

6. George Nixon, Ottawa, to Smith, 13 Sept. 1950; Box 3, MG 5, Series 2, File 1, SSMPL.

7. Privy Council order 1118.

8. Nixon to Smith, 21 March 1951; Box 3, MG 5, Series 2, File 1, SSMPL.

9. Smith to Nixon, 26 March 1951; Box 3, MG 5, Series 2, File 1, SSMPL.

10. Smith to Nixon, 8 Jan. 1949; Box 3, MG 5, Series 2, Box 3, File 1, SSMPL.

11. Nixon to Mackinnon, 1 Feb. 1949; Box 3, MG 5, Series 2, File 1, SSMPL.

12. Smith to Nixon, 5 Aug. 1950; Box 3, MG 5, Series 2, File 1, SSMPL.

13. Smith to Nixon, 26 March 1951; Box 3, MG 5, Series 2, File 1, SSMPL.

14. Winters to Nixon, 11 April 1951 and Nixon to Smith, 26 April 1951; Box 3, MG 5, Series 2, File 1, SSMPL.

15. Smith to Nixon, 28 Jan. 1953; Box 3, MG 5, Series 2, File 1, SSMPL.

16. Undated Speech in Box 3, MG 5, Series 1, File 2, SSMPL.

17. Smith received a copy of Norman Riddiough's article, "Penetang Sees Its Dream Come True as Result of Investment of Only $7,500," as it was reprinted in the *Sun Times* of Owen Sound, 9 October 1954.

18. Smith to Sprague, 15 Nov. 1954 and Sprague to Smith, 22 November 1954; Box 3, MG 5, Series 2, File 1, SSMPL.

19. Smith to Landon, 20 Oct. 1954; Box 3, MG 5, Series 2, File 1, SSMPL.

20. Landon to Smith, 5 Nov. 1954; Box 3, MG 5, Series 2, File 1, SSMPL.

21. Smith to May, n.d., Box 3, MG 5, Series 2, File 1, SSMPL.

22. Smith to the Deputy Minister, Travel and Publicity, 18 Oct. 1954; Box 3, MG 5, Series 2, File 1, SSMPL.

23. Deputy Minister (Crowe) to Smith, 22 Oct. 1954, and Smith to the Deputy Minister, 16 Nov. 1954; Box 3, MG 5, Series 2, File 1, SSMPL.

24. Smith to Crowe, 16 Nov. 1954; Box 3, MG 5, Series 2, File 1, SSMPL.

25. There is an undated note with the names of J. Herbert, Chief, Historical Sites Division, National Parks Branch, Department of Northern Affairs and Natural Resources;

Mr. Coleman, Director of the National Parks Branch, Department of Northern Affairs and Natural Resources; Box 3, MG 5, Series 2, File 1, SSMPL.

26. Smith to Henry Lang, 14 June 1961; Box 3, MG 5, Series 2, File 1, SSMPL.

27. Lang to Dinsdale, Ottawa, 10 Aug. 1961; Box 3, MG 5, Series 2, File 1, SSMPL.

28. For further information about the reconstruction of Fort St. Joseph, see Stephen L. Cumbaa, *A Study of Military and Civilian Food Remains from Fort St. Joseph, Ontario (1795–1838)* (Ottawa: Zooarchaeological Identification Centre, National Museum of Natural Sciences, 1979); Helen Devereux, "A Preliminary Report: The Excavaton of Fort St. Joseph, 1963," unpublished manuscript of the Department of Anthopology, University of Toronto, prepared for The National Historic Sites Division, Department of Northern Affairs and Natural Resources, 1 March 1965; Fred C. Hamil, "An Early Settlement on St. Joseph Island," *Ontario History*, LIII, 4 (Dec. 1961); Herman Dunlap Smith, *The Desbarats Country* (Chicago: Privately printed, 1950). See also H. Lambart's 1963 Memorandum to Mr. A.J.H. Richardson of the Department of Northern Affairs: "Concerning References to Fort St. Joseph from Historic Documents"; SSMPL.

Bibliography

PRIMARY SOURCES

Bartlett, Ruhl. *The Record of American Diplomacy*. New York: Knopf, 1964. (A collection of US treaties and diplomatic correspondence.)

The Boston Sentinel, 1812.

Glyn Smith Collection, Sault Ste. Marie (Ontario) Public Library.

Innis, Mary Quayle (ed). *Mrs. Simcoe's Diary*. New York: St. Martin Press, 1965.

The John Askin Papers, 1796–1820, vol. II.. Detroit: Burton Historical Collection, 1931.

Michigan Pioneer and Historical Collection. Lansing: Darius D. Thorp, State Printer and Binder, 1889.

The Montreal Gazette. 1794–1812.

National Archives of Canada, R.G. 8

US Congress, *Debates and Proceedings*, Thirteenth Congress–Third Session, 1815.

UNPUBLISHED GOVERNMENT PAPERS

Allen, Robert S. *A History of the British Indian Department in North America (1755–1830)*. Ottawa: Department of Indian Affairs and Northern Development, Manuscript Report No. 109, Dec. 1971.

Carter-Edwards, Dennis. *The 41st (the Welsh) Regiment, 1700–1815*. Ottawa: Parks Canada, 1986.

Cumbaa, Stephen L. *A Study of Military and Civilian Food Remains from Fort St. Joseph, Ontario (1795–1828)*. Ottawa: Zooarchaeological Identification Centre, National Museum of Natural Sciences, 31 March 1979.

Devereux, Helen. "A Preliminary Report: The Excavation of Fort St. Joseph, 1963", unpublished manuscript of the Department of Anthropology, University of Toronto, prepared for the Naitonal Historic Sites Division, Department of Northern Affairs and Natural Resources, 1 March 1965.

Fort St. Joseph, National Historic Site, Management Plan, Public Open House, 16 June 1998, Canadian Heritage, Parks Canada.

Karrow, P.F. *Quarternary Geology, St. Joseph Island.* Toronto: Ministry of Northern Development and Mines, Ontario Geological Survey, Open File Report 5809.

Vincent, Elizabeth. *Fort St. Joseph: A History.* Ottawa: Parks Canada, 1978.

PUBLISHED SECONDARY SOURCES

Allen, Robert S. "His Majesty's Indian Allies: Native Peoples, the British Crown and the War of 1812," *Michigan Historical Review*, XIV, 2 (Fall, 1988), pp. 1–14.

Armour, David A. (ed.) *Massacre at Mackinac: Alexander Henry's Travels and Adventures in Canada and the Indian Territories between the Years 1760 and 1764.* Mackinac Island: State Park Commission, 1966.

Althoff, Gerry T. "Oliver Hazard Perry and the Battle of Lake Erie," *Michigan Historical Review,* XIV, 2 (Fall, 1988), pp. 25–57.

Ashley, Kathryne Belden. *Islands of the Manitou.* Sault Ste. Marie, Mich.: Lake Superior State College, n.d.

Bayliss, Joseph and Estelle. *Historic St. Joseph Island.* Cedar Rapids, Iowa: The Torch Press, 1938.

Bemis, S.F. *Jay's Treaty: A Study in Commerce and Diplomacy.* New York: Macmillan, 1924 [1923].

✓Berton, Pierre. *Flames across the Border.* Toronto: McClelland and Stewart, 1981.

✓Berton, Pierre. *The Invasion of Canada.* Toronto: McClelland and Stewart, 1980.

Bowen, Phoebe-May. "The Battle of Lake Erie in the War of 1812," *Inland Seas*, XLIII, 3 (Fall 1987), pp. 178–187.

Burt, A.L. *The United States, Great Britain, and British North America*. Toronto: Ryerson, 1966 [1940].

Carter-Edwards, Dennis. "The War of 1812 along the Detroit Frontier: A Canadian Perspective," *Michigan Historical Review*, XIII, 2 (Fall, 1987), pp. 25–50.

Catton, Bruce. *Michigan: A Bicentennial History*. New York: W.W. Norton, 1976.

Cleland, Charles E. *The Prehistoric Animal Ecology and Ethnozoology of the Upper Great Lakes Region*. Ann Arbor: University of Michigan Press, Anthropological Papers, Museum of Anthropology, No. 29, 1966.

Coffin, William F. *1812: The War and its Moral: A Canadian Chronicle*. Montreal: John Lovell, 1864.

Coles, Harry L. *The War of 1812*. Chicago: University of Chicago Press, 1965.

Calloway, Colin G. "The End of an Era: British-Indian Relations in the Great Lakes Region after the War of 1812," *Michigan Historical Review*, XII, 2 (Fall 1986), pp. 1–20.

Cook, Samuel F. *Drummond Island: The Story of the British Occupation, 1815–1828*. Lansing, Mich.: 1896.

Dictionary of Canadian Biography, 1000–1700. Toronto: University of Toronto Press, vol. I.

Dunbar, Willis F. *Michigan: A History of the Wolverine State*. Grand Rapids: Eerdmans, 1965.

Dunnigan, Brian Leigh. *King's Men at Mackinac: The British Garrisons, 1780–1796*. Mackinac Island: State Park Commission, 1973.

Ellis, Chris J., and Deller, D. Brian. *The Archaeology of Southern Ontario to A.D. 1650*. London, Ontario: Occasional Publications of the London Chapter, Ontario Archaeological Society, Publication No. 5, 1990.

Ferguson, William. *Scotland's Relations with England: A Survey to 1707*. Edinburgh: John Donald, 1977.

Fitting, James E. *The Archaeology of Michigan: A Guide to the Prehistory of the Great Lakes Region*. Bloomfield Hills, Michigan: Cranbrook Institute of Science, 1975.

Fuller, George N. *Michigan: A Centennial History of the State and its People*. Chicago: Lewis, 1939, 2 vols.

Goodrich, Calvin. *The First Michigan Frontier*. Ann Arbor: University of Michigan Press, 1940.

Hamil, Fred C. "An Early Settlement on St. Joseph Island," *Ontario History*, LIII, 4 (Dec. 1961).

Hamil, Fred C. "Michigan in the War of 1812," *Michigan History*, XLIV, 3 (Sept. 1960), pp. 260–269.

Hammond, M.O. *Canadian Footprints*. Toronto: Macmillan, 1926.

Hanna, Margaret G., and Kooyman, Brian. *Approaches to Algonquian History*. Calgary: University of Calgary Archaeological Association, 1982.

✓ Hannay, James. *History of the War of 1812*. Toronto: Morang & Co., 1905.

Harris, R. Cole (ed.), and Matthews, Geoffrey J. (cartographer/designer). *Historical Atlas of Canada.* Toronto: University of Toronto Press, 1987.

Havighurst, Walter. *Three Flags at the Straits: The Forts of Mackinac.* Englewood Cliffs, N.J.: Prentice-Hall, 1966.

Hickey, Donald R. "Federalist Party Unity and the War of 1912," *Journal of American Studies*, XII, 1 (April 1978), pp. 23–39.

Hinsperger, *Stories of the Past: 300 Years of Soo History.* N.p. 1967.

Hitsman, J. Mackay. *The Incredible War of 1812: A Military History.* Toronto: University of Toronto Press, 1965.

Horsman, Reginald. "On to Canada: Manifest Destiny and United States Strategy in the War of 1812," *Michigan Historical Review*, XIII, 2 (Fall 1987), pp. 1–24.

Howell, William Maher. "The Arrival of Dobbins at Erie," *Inland Seas*, LI, 2 (Summer 1995), pp. 32–34.

Lee, Ellen R. "A Research Model for Extracting Interactive Patterns at a Fur Trade Post on the Upper Great Lakes: Fort St. Joseph, Ontario, 1796–1829," MA Thesis, University of Manitoba, 1986.

Malcomson, Bob. "War on the Lakes," *The Beaver* (April/May 1990), pp. 44–52.

Martin, Susan Rapalje. "A Reconsideration of Aboriginal Fishing Strategies in the Northern Great Lakes Region", *American Antiquity*, LIV, 3 (1989).

May, George S. *War of 1812*. Mackinac Island: State Park Commission.

Mount, Graeme S., Abbott, John, and Mulloy, Michael J. *The Border at Sault Ste. Marie*. Toronto: Dundurn, 1995.

Perkins, Bradford (ed.). *The Causes of the War of 1812: National Honor or National Interest?* New York: Holt, Rinehart and Winston, 1962.

Petersen, Eugene T. *Mackinac Island: Its History in Pictures*. Mackinac Island: State Park Commission, 1973.

Rogers, Edward S., and Smith, Donald. *Aboriginal Ontario: Historical Perspectives on the First Nations*. Toronto: Dundurn, 1994.

Sheppard, George. *Plunder, Profit, and Paroles: A Social History of the War of 1812 in Upper Canada*. Montreal: McGill-Queen's University Press, 1994.

Smith, Herman Dunlap. *The Desbarats Country*. Chicago: Privately printed, 1950.

Stacey, C.P. "Upper Canada at War, 1814: Captain Armstrong Reports," *Ontario History*, XLVIII (1956), pp. 37–42.

Stacey, C.P. *The Undefended Border: The Myth and The Reality*. Ottawa: Canadian Historical Association, No. 1, 1953.

Stacey, C.P. "The War of 1812 in Canadian History," *Ontario History*, L (1958), pp. 153–159.

Stagg, J.C.A. *Mr. Madison's War*. Princeton: Princeton University Press, 1983.

White, Patrick C.T. *A Nation on Trial: America and the War of 1812*. New York: Wiley, 1965.

Stanley, G.F.G., "The Indians in the War of 1812," *Canadian Historical Review*, XXXI (1950), pp. 145–165.

Stanley, G.F.G. *The War of 1812: Land Operations*. Toronto: Macmillan, 1983.

Stanley, G.F.G. "The Significance of Six Nations Participation in the War of 1812," *Ontario History*, LV (1963).

Strang, James. *Ancient and Modern Michilimackinac*. Mackinac Island: State Park Commission, 1973.

Van Fleet, M.A. *Old and New Mackinac*. Cincinnati: Western Methodist Book Concern, 1974.

Whate, Ron. "Frontier-Post Pearlware: Ceramics recovered at the 'Siberia of the North,'" *National Parks Centennial* (July–Aug. 1985), pp. 37–41.

Widder, Keith R. *Reveillé Till Taps: Soldier Life at Fort Mackinac, 1780–1895*. Mackinac Island: State Park Commission, 1972.

Williams, Meade C. *Early Mackinac: An Historical and Descriptive Sketch*. St. Louis: Buschart Bros. Print, 1903.

Woltz, L. Oughtred. "The Chippewa Cession of Mackinac to George III, May 12, 1781," *Michigan History*, IX, 2 (April 1925), pp. 136–142.

Yarnell, Richard Asa. *Aboriginal Relationships between Culture and Plant Life in the Great Lakes Region*. Ann Arbor: University of Michigan Press, Anthropological Papers, Museum of Anthropology, No. 23, 1964.

Index